WINGS OF COURAGE

Wings of Courage

FEMINIST CONSCIOUSNESS IN THE SELECT TEXTS OF BUCHI EMECHETA AND FLORA NWAPA

Anupama L,

SMART MOVES

Contents

Book Title: Wings of Courage: Feminist Consciousness in the Select Texts of Buchi Emecheta and Flora Nwapa
Book Author: Anupama L,
Published by SMART MOVES
E 5/11, 2nd Floor, Bitten Market
Bhopal-462038
India

Printed and bound by SMART MOVES
E 5/11, 2nd Floor, Bitten Market
Bhopal-462038
India
p-ISBN: 978-81-940996-7-3
e-ISBN: 978-81-940996-6-6

This edition published in: 2019 ISBN (ISBN Pending)

Acknowledgements

I am extremely grateful to my mother Lalitha Bhai, father R. Vijaya Raghavan, husband Dr. J Dasan and my son, Vaishnav for the successful completion of this book. It is their constant support, prayers and encouragement that helped me to finalize this book.

I record my sincere thanks to the Principal of All Saints' College, Dr. Caroline Beena Mendez, the Head of the Department of English, Ms. Sonya J. Nair, Dr. Sr. Pascola D'Souza, Sr. Nancy and all the other teachers in the Department of English for their help and encouragement. I sincerely thank Ms. Khyrunnisa A, author of children's fiction, speaker, writer and former Associate Professor in English at All Saints' College for her continuous support and motivation.

I express my gratitude to the staff of the State Central Public Library, Kerala University library and All Saints' College library for their help and support. With all my heart, I thank Almighty God whose grace illuminates every page.

Preface

Buchi Emecheta's *Second-Class Citizen* (1974), *The Joys of Motherhood* (1979) and Flora Nwapa's *Efuru* (1966) are texts that can be read in the light of feminist literary theories. These texts were selected as it dealt with the obstacles and oppression that Nigerian women encountered in their lives. These texts attack patriarchy and examine the personal from black women's point of view. These selected texts attempts to cleanse the society that upholds patriarchy and analyze the situation of black women from their own point of view. Both fictional and autobiographical elements in these texts serve to highlight the experiences of different black women and expose the various ways by which women are affected by race, gender, culture and tradition. The focus of the book is on the lived experiences of black women in Nigeria. An attempt is made to analyze the lives of black women as is seen by the Nigerian women writers, Buchi Emecheta and Flora Nwapa.

The selected novelists outline the changes in the social and cultural arenas due to the spread of western education and Christianity. Both *Efuru* and *The Joys of Motherhood* portray the ostracization of the childless women prevalent in the community. *Efuru* analyzes the western influence on traditional Igbo beliefs and customs. Efuru, the protagonist is not shattered for being childless. She emerges as an independent woman, creates new identity and spiritually nurtures her community. Emecheta's *The Joys of Motherhood* does not glorify motherhood. Children do not necessarily have a loving relationship with their mothers. Emecheta states in the novel, "the joy of being a mother is the joy of giving all to your children" (219). The title of the novel is taken from Flora Nwapa's *Efuru* and sounds bitterly ironic. *The Joys of Motherhood* is her most complex novel where she differs from the existing socio-political and cultural imperatives. She uses literary devices like flash back, interior monologue and bildungsroman. In this novel she deals with several issues like the problems of polygamy, motherhood and situation of widows and childless women. While male writers like Chinua Achebe portray mother with reverence, Buchi Emecheta presents the problems and chaos involved in a mother's life.

Nnu Ego, the central character in Emecheta's *The Joys of Motherhood* realizes that children do not always bring fulfillment. As Marie A. Umeh points out in "The Joys of Motherhood: Myth or Reality?"

> What Emecheta does is to present an African woman's reaction to a universal problem. Children often fail to honour their parents. In voicing this idea through the traditionalist, Nnu Ego, Emecheta emphasizes the fact that women have the social responsibility to criticize and participate in the social order (41).

Nnu Ego evolves from a staunch traditionalist to a feminist as she realizes her second class status. As Umeh states,

> The ironies and cruelties of her life force the protagonist to move from the collective consciousness to the individual consciousness ... Like her spokesperson, the narrator, Nnu Ego having found a place for herself in the new order of female emancipation divorces herself from the traditional African concepts in her search for abundant life" (43).

Finally she realizes that sacrificing friends and comforts of life for her sons were mistakes. Sometimes Emecheta personally identifies with the character as when she says, "The men make it look as if we must aspire for children or die" (187).

Second-Class Citizen successfully depicts the protagonist Adah's growth from a naïve young girl to her final stage of self-realization and independence. The novel discusses the numerous struggles of Adah as a mother, wife and as a migrant. Though she faces racism in London, her husband, Francis is her major opponent. The novel describes her life in a foreign land with an inconsiderate and selfish husband. Katherine Frank asserts that "the best place to approach Emecheta's fiction is with neither her first nor her last book, but with *Second-Class Citizen*" (479).

All these selected texts throw light on women's dreams, their ability to master pain and betrayal with courage and their capacities to evolve into strong independent women. The women characters in these novels like Efuru, Adah, Nnu Ego and Adaku assert the needs of both collective and individual female identity within their culture. These women transcend the barriers imposed by the traditional Igbo society though Nnu Ego becomes a rebel only after her death. They participate fully as human beings for the welfare of their community instead of confining themselves to their roles of daughters, wives and mothers.

Introduction

This section looks into the realistic and fictional experiences in the selected texts of the black women writers Buchi Emecheta and Flora Nwapa, the major themes in the selected literary texts, the status accorded to women in the pre-colonial, colonial and in the post-colonial Africa, and the impact of racism and slavery faced by the blacks in Africa. The selected texts represent the experiences and developing identities of Nigerian women. These texts present a different world with quite different standards from those that the reader might be familiar with.

The texts selected for the study are Flora Nwapa's *Efuru* and Buchi Emecheta's *Second-Class Citizen* and *The Joys of Motherhood*. These texts have both fictional and autobiographical elements. Many recent literary works represent the slippage between fiction and autobiography. Literary works like Norma Kouri's *Honor Lost: Love and Death in Modern day Jordan* (2003), James Frey's *A Million Little Pieces* (2003) and Helen Demidenko's *The Hand that Signed the Paper* (1994) are examples of works that were originally regarded as autobiography but later came to be known as fictional works. Both Buchi Emecheta and Flora Nwapa serve as agents of change and beacon of hope for thousands of oppressed black women. Apart from narrating the authors' own experiences, their works reflect the violent suppression that numerous black women encounter in their lives.

Both Nwapa and Emecheta write about issues and concerns in the lives of Igbo women affected by British colonialism. Their literary works examine the features of Igbo culture, women's wish for change and their desire to be accepted within their community. These texts place an emphasis on women as individual and analyses the impact of western education on their beliefs and values. The women characters evolve as the novels progress. They attain self-realization and become increasingly independent.

This book attempts to analyze the situation of black women based on Buchi Emecheta's *Second Class Citizen, The Joys of Motherhood* and Flora Nwapa's *Efuru.* These texts are authentic as they are based on the true life experiences of black women. The selected texts draw on the real experiences of the writers as well as the experiences of numerous other black women living in similar circumstances whom these writers encounter within their community. Commenting on the writings of black women, Houston Baker critically observes "To understand our origins we must journey through different straits and in the end we may only find confusion" (Baker 1).

Emecheta's *Second-Class Citizen* narrates the struggle and survival of the protagonist, Adah. Her shift from Nigeria to England is marked by deterioration in her status from high class position to a low class position. In England, she faces racism and struggles hard both as mother and wife. Like Adah, Buchi Emecheta who was born in Nigeria, near Lagos moved to England with her two children and her husband. Emecheta succeeded in graduating from London University with a degree in Sociology. The novel depicts her struggle to survive in a hostile white European society with a jealous and abusive husband.

Emecheta's other novel that is selected for the study is *The Joys of Motherhood* which deals with the life of the protagonist, Nnu Ego. Nnu Ego is the daughter of the great chief and elephant hunter, Agbadi and the proud Ona. Nnu Ego's first husband sent her back to her father's village because she was childless. Though Agbadi is reluctant to arrange a remarriage he allows Nnu Ego to marry Nnaife Owulum. Nnaife worked as a laundry man in the home of an English family. Although it was a loveless marriage, Nnu Ego is comforted by the fact that she has several children. Motherhood is a major theme of the novel. As she bathed her baby son, Oshia she reflects, "She was now sure as she bathed her baby son and cooked for her husband, that her old age would be happy, that when she died there would be somebody left behind to refer to her as 'mother'" (54). Ultimately Nnu Ego regrets being a mother having so many children because they seemed to have little concern for her well-being.

The impact of colonialism is also dealt with in the novel. Nigerian culture is affected by capitalism and western notions of religion and education. The effects harm both individuals and societies. Nnu Ego's tragic situation is due to the fact that she could not embrace change. Several people adapt themselves to the foreign beliefs and traditions while several others could not. For instance, Oshia makes a break with tradition when he decides to accept a scholarship to study in the US. Her second son, Adim too discards tradition and pursues a path much like Oshia. Nnu Ego's daughter, Kehinde too refuses to obey tradition. She wanted to marry the man of her choice and asserts her right to happiness. But Nnu Ego who is unwilling to accept change remains broken and alone. Another novel that is selected for the study is Flora Nwapa's *Efuru*. The title character Efuru is a strong, successful woman in her West African village. Efuru elopes with Adizua before Adizua could pay her bride price. After a few years a daughter is born to Efuru. Adizua begins disappearing for days at a time and finally deserts Efuru and marries another woman. Efuru's child too dies and she returns to her father. Later Efuru marries a man named Eneberi. As Efuru is childless, Eneberi too deserts her and the same tragedy is repeated again in her life. Efuru is left alone, childless, husbandless and without family. Finally she lives happily among her people. She helps them in their needs and worships the goddess of the lake, Uhamiri who gives her wealth and happiness.

But Uhamiri couldn't give her children as she herself was childless.

The book is divided into three chapters. The first chapter titled, 'Journey towards Liberation: A Review of Black Feminist Literary Theory' deals with a brief discussion of black feminism as it is imperative while examining the issues posed in the texts of Nigerian women writers, Buchi Emecheta and Flora Nwapa. The second chapter, 'Representation of Women in Buchi Emecheta's *Second-Class Citizen* and *The Joys of Motherhood*' analyzes the representation of African women in Buchi Emecheta's selected texts. It studies the evolution of consciousness of the female protagonists, Adah and Nnu Ego and also discusses the various modes of protests adopted by the women characters. The third chapter, 'Locating the Self in Flora Nwapa's *Efuru*' discusses the protagonist Efuru's role and place in a changing society. It examines the way in which Efuru reclaims a space for herself in the African society.

A brief survey of early African literature can be beneficial as it can throw light on the present day realities that African women encounter in their lives. Much of the earlier African literature was written in the post-independence era and dealt with the impact of colonization. The postcolonial scenario marked by the exploitation of blacks by blacks is a major theme in later African writing. African women are not adequately represented in these works and their social and economic status was reduced as a result of colonization. In modern African societies where women have minimal power, they are subject to tremendous institutional and interpersonal violence. Women have almost no power over their own lives. This reality is authentically portrayed in African fictional works. These works highlight the status of African women in the pre-colonial, colonial and postcolonial situations. They expose the suffering of African women following the imposition of colonial ideology and Victorian attitudes. Due to the colonization women lost her earlier elite status. This caused the further subjugation of women who were viewed as sexual objects and prostitutes.

Even white male anthropologists accept the fact that black women were more oppressed than their white counterparts. White women viewed them as menial creatures and as beasts of burden. Though both Western and African feminists deal with issues of gender and the status of women as 'second class citizen', African women's experiences are different from those of Western women and the Western model cannot be used to evaluate African literature.

Under the influence of colonization, the colonized became passive victims and black women made little progress. The colonizers exploited the natives by extracting their wealth and utilizing their labor. The colonized became the producers and consumers of commodities and served the need of the colonizers for both raw materials and markets. Women lost their power, wealth, and the rights that they had enjoyed earlier. In the colonial society men were more privileged than women. Generally native men handled the technological inventions of the colonizers and had more access to money. Women were economically dependent on them and this lead to the patriarchal nuclear family. Women too seized the available opportunities to work as laborers. Women attained their social and economic security through men. They were subjected to sexual and economic exploitation by the colonizers.

By the late nineteenth century European powers struggled to gain control of Africa. Colonial administration was imposed and relations between men and women were disturbed. Studies on African women reflect male bias. Roopali Sircar in her *The Twice Colonized: Women in African Literature* cites Kenneth Little whose study on the African urban woman is dominated by mistresses, concubines, prostitutes, outside wives and disgruntled spouses" (3). Critical works by Westerners also reflect their attitude to African women. Nancy J. Hafkins and Edna G. Bay in *Women in Africa: Studies in Social and Economic Change* arrive at the conclusion that in African societies, the position of women is similar to that of domestic animals. The work describes queens, amazons and matriarchs in the traditional African matriarchal society. It stresses the need for African women's economic and political independence.

Early African societies were hunting and gathering societies. Men were employed in hunting and women in gathering vegetable products. Boserup in 1970 referred to Africa as "the region of female farming par excellence" (Sircar 23). Studies reveal that in hunting and gathering societies women were essentially the equals of men. In pre-colonial societies women were more powerful than is usually assumed. Roopali Sircar writes:

> Recent studies suggest (i) that women exercised political power more frequently than was formally assumed, and (ii) that although the symbolic expression of women's power differed from those of men's, women were not necessarily considered to be less powerful. (24)

During the period of colonization, African men and women suffered the violence of enslavement. Slavery as defined by the Slavery Convention of 1926 is "the status or condition of a person over whom any or all of the powers attaching to the rights of ownership are exercised" and a slave is a "person who is wholly or partly owned by another person or organization" (*International Encyclopedia of Women* vol. 4: 1855-56). Bales in *Disposable People: New Slavery in Global Economy* states that towards the end of the twentieth century there were approximately 27 million people in slavery and slave like conditions. Slavery affects the people working as domestic servants, prostitutes, and those held as bonded laborers. Slavery also occurs within the framework of marriage. Women are physically as well as emotionally exploited in slavery.

Slavery involves a theft of the body. The captive body is severed from its motive will and desire. Both male and female bodies are reduced to objects for the captor. The captive body is regarded as 'other' marked by sheer physical powerlessness. It is a crime against the black Africans.

Their bodies were stolen by the European powers.

Hortense Spillers in her essay "Mama's Baby, Papa's May be" quotes William Goodell; "the smack of the whip is all day long in the ears of those who are on the plantation, or in the vicinity; and it is used with such dexterity and severity as not only to lacerate the skin but to tear out small portions of the flesh at almost every stake" (James and Sharpley-Whiting 61). Spillers says that the "anatomical specifications of rupture, of altered human tissue, take on the objective description of laboratory prose – eyes beaten out, arms, backs, skulls branded, a left jaw, a right ankle, calculated work of iron, whips, chains, knives, the canine patrol, the bullet" (61). African females were physically and mentally violated. They were the victims of rape and the targets of brutality and torture by males.

The position of blacks in a white world was no better than that of animals. In *The American Slave Code in Theory and Practice shown by its Statutes, Judicial Decisions and Illustrative Facts,* Goodell cites an advertisement from Charleston Mercury on 12 October 1838:

> To planters and others - Wanted, Fifty Negros, any person, having sick Negros, considered incurable by their respective physicians, and wishing to dispose of them, Dr. S. will pay cash for Negroes affected with scrofula, or Kings Evil, confirmed hypochondriasm, apoplexy, diseases of the liver, kidneys, spleen, stomach and intestines, bladder and its appendages, diarrhoea, dysentery, etc. The *highest cash price will be paid*, on application as above at No. 110 Church Street, Charleston [Goodell's Emphasis]. (James and Sharpley-Whiting 62)

> The blacks were not regarded as human beings. The "entire captive community becomes a living laboratory", as Spillers says (63).

Rachel Bowlby analyses the problem of slavery in "Breakfast in America: Uncle Tom's Cultural Histories", one of the articles in *Nation and Narration,* edited by Homi K Bhabha. Topsy in *Uncle Tom's Cabin* is introduced as a present from Saint Clare, a New Orleans slave holder to his New England cousin Miss Ophelia. The child is a "fresh- caught specimen" "for you to educate" (200). The novel provoked anti-slavery movements and had a leading place in publishing history and Stowe herself claimed, "God wrote it" (199). In 1863, Abraham Lincoln called Harriet Beecher Stowe "the little woman who made the big war" (199). Cora Kaplan in the editor's introduction to *Aurora Leigh and Other Poems* cites Elizabeth Barrett Browning's defense of Stowe's *Uncle Tom's Cabin.* Bowlby quotes the passage:

> Oh, and is it possible that you think a woman has no business with questions like the question of slavery? Then she had better use a pen no more. She had better subside into slavery and concubinage herself, I think, as in the times of old, shut herself up with the Penelopes in the 'women's apartment', and take no rank among thinkers and speakers. (182)

Topsy lacks the ability of interpretation and must be given a meaning for everything. "You'll have to give her a meaning, or she'll make one", says St. Clare (201). Stowe's novel is an attempt to provide the meaning. The contrast between Topsy and St. Clare's daughter Little Eva is depicted in racial terms:

> There stood the two children representative of the two extremes of society. The fair, hybrid child, with her golden head, her deep eyes, her spiritual, noble brow and prince like movements; and her black, keen, subtle cringing, yet acute neighbour. They stood the representatives of their races. The Saxons born of ages of cultivation, command, education, physical and

moral eminence; the African, born of ages of submission, ignorance, toil and vice. (200)

The racial distinctions were made by the whites. Stowe appeals for a common humanity rooted in Christian belief. When Topsy is asked to confess a crime which she had not committed, she confesses because "Why, Missis said I must 'fess" (361). When Topsy was asked about her mother and her birth place she says "Never had none!" "Never was born!" " ... I spect I grow'd" (201).

The concept of slavery makes Augustine St. Clare speculate, "I wonder, now, if I was divided up and inventoried ... how much I might bring. Say so much for the shape of my head, so much for a high forehead, so much for education, learning, talent, honesty, religion!" (204). Hortense J. Spillers in "Mama's Baby, Papa's May be" refers to the slaves as 'cargo' that bled, packed like so many live sardines among immovable object.

The color of the skin was a decisive factor in human dealings. The white skinned captors paid no attention to the relationships of the blacks. Mothers were separated from children, husbands from wives and brothers from sisters. Blacks were 'ugly' and 'hideous'. There is evidence to prove that men outnumbered women on slave ships bound for America from Africa. The captives were 'quantities'. Though they were not regarded as humans, the slave vessel is ironically referred to as 'she'. There are no written records on the condition of captive females. Spillers notes that the sexual violation of captive females and their rage against their oppressors were insignificant events to the captains and their crew. The opening chapter of bell hooks', *Ain't I a woman? Black Women and Feminism* addresses the problem of female captives and the unborn children. Feminists try to unveil this silence that is due to distortion.

The offspring of the captive females were in the position of orphans. The 'owner' is the all-powerful possessor. But the child is unrelated to both its mother and the owner. Slavery generates only property relations and no kinship relation can exist. In Spillers' essay, she refers to the experiences of Frederick Douglass thus, "For what this separation is (sic) done, I do not know, unless it is to hinder the development of the child's affection towards its mother, and to blunt and destroy the natural affection of the mother for the child. This is the inevitable result" (James and Sharpley-Whiting 75). Further, "the early separation of us from our mother had well-nigh blotted the fact of our relationships from our memories" (76).

If kinship relations existed, property relations would be undermined since the offspring would then 'belong' to a mother and a father. The slave-owner relationship will not be possible in such a situation. The African American woman is denied parental rights. The enslaved females were beasts of burden who increased their owner's stock.

In the case of several black women, marriage is a form of slavery, often without their consent. Most often women are married at an early age resulting in serious health problems. In the *International Encyclopedia of women*, Carron Somerset refers to Sawyer who in *Slavery in the Twentieth century* quotes Montgomery's definition of servile marriages as "any institution whereby a woman without the rights to refuse is promised or given in marriage, on payment of a consideration in money or in kind, or may be transferred to another person or on death of her husband may be inherited by another person" (1856). Women's sexual and reproductive powers are under the control of their husbands. If the husband dies the wives of the dead husband (in case of polygynous marriages) are inherited by husband's brother. Such marriages are a violation of human rights.

Early marriage of the girl child is prompted by several reasons, which include easing the burden of one child, making use of the bride-price to repay debts, and marrying a girl off before she loses her virginity. In many marriages women have to suffer painful forced sex. Through marriage they undergo physical, mental, emotional and economic exploitation.

According to feminist critics 'sexual slavery' refers to situations in which men use women and children in conditions of slavery. Insecurity and exploitation in marriage lead many women into prostitution. In the 1920s and 1930s feminists in The British Commonwealth League worked against 'sexual slavery'. They opposed prostitution, child marriage and the buying and selling of women in marriage. Men earned money and they owned women. Women were not viewed as persons but as commodities. Female sexual slavery can involve marital rape, father-daughter and brother-sister incest, bride price, selling of the female child and prostitution. Kathleen Barry, founder of Coalition Against Trafficking in Women (CATW) applied the term 'sexual slavery' to prostitution in *Female Sexual Slavery* (1979).

International Encyclopedia of Women defines prostitution as "the provision of sexual service in exchange for material gains" (1678). Prostitution arises from women's subordination. Men exploit women's subordinate status and their economic disadvantage and their victimization by other men. *The Encyclopedia* cites Reynolds's view that between 1451 and 1810 approximately 7,525,600 slaves were imported into the Americas and the Atlantic basin. Women had a status inferior to all men and so they were subjected to sexual and economic exploitation. Women in plantations were forced to do hard fieldwork. Black men who enjoyed a comparatively higher status were given jobs as skilled craftsman. The purchase price of women slaves was lower than that of males.

In 1926, the Slavery Convention of the League of Nations was set up to abolish slave trade. The Universal Declaration of Human Rights, 1948, states:

"Article 1 – All human beings are born free and equal in dignity

and rights. [...]
Article 4 – No one shall be held in slavery and the slave trade shall
be prohibited in all their forms. [...]
Article 23 (1) – Everyone has the right to the free choice of employment, to just and favorable conditions of work and to protection against unemployment" (1856).

The Convention for the Suppression of the Traffic in Persons and the Exploitation of the Prostitution of Others was introduced in 1949. This was followed by the United Nations' Convention on the Abolition of Slavery the Slave Trade and Institutions and Practices. There is evidence to prove that despite all this millions of people are still held in servitude.

Apart from the oppression due to colonization and slavery, African women also suffered within their families. The concept of family in Africa is different from that in the West. Traditionally there are different types of families in Africa. The father is an outsider in a Asanti family. The family consists of mother, her children and her brother. If the biological mother of the child dies, there are many others who assumed the role of the mother. Even a male can be regarded as 'mother'. A child called all his mother's sisters and mother's brothers 'mother' because they fulfill the obligations of the mother. To the child, 'mother' is not an individual but a group of persons (Turnbill 137). The African family is basically an economic unit. Economic relationships, which are necessary for the survival of society, are found in familial relationships too. Married adult sons remain in their father's compounds and the family is large and polygynous.

Women were stronger in traditional African families. Women had control over economic resources and a mother had a higher status in the family. In a polygynous family a man has several wives. The senior wife is respected by all. She is the manager who controls the rest of the women. Elder women were also respected. Youth was associated with powerlessness and age with power. It was considered a shame for a man if he could not respect the mother of his children.

Marriages could be either *nilotic* or *interlacustrine.* Bride price was paid to the bride's people in return for her services and her sexual power, which were surrendered to the man. A biological father can claim to be the father of an illegitimate child only by paying compensation to the women's male relatives who looked after the child. Divorce was complicated because the bride price was non-refundable as the woman rendered services to her husband's household. After marriage the women's relations with her father's household weakened. Widows were inherited by a brother or the son of another wife of the deceased. Polygamy was common in African societies. In interlacustrine marriage, low bride price was paid. The husband and his close kinsman had sexual rights over the woman.

Colonization had its impact on African families. Colonialism affected marriage systems. Christians and Muslims registered their marriages. Marriages in churches and mosques were regarded as respectable. John V. Taylor in *The Growth of the Church in Uganda: An Attempt at Understanding* claims that all people not married in church were regarded as "living in sin" (123) though their married life may be stable. They were automatically excommunicated and the women so married were referred to as 'malaya' (prostitutes). The Catholic Church did not permit divorce and the African Church did not allow remarriage after divorce. Women favored a polygamous marriage because women had more liberty as the man could not, obviously, control all his wives.

In African societies, women have significant roles as wives and mothers. African literary works reveal the joys of motherhood and the agony at the denial of motherhood. A man's lineage is maintained only by the reproductive capacities of his wives. In almost all African fictional works, the mother is the most significant character. All other women are pale and insignificant. Attempts are made to appease the gods to achieve motherhood. The sufferings of women are mainly for their children.

Polygamy, female circumcision, women's subversion techniques and the impact of motherhood on the lives of women are some of the major themes discussed by black women writers.

In *So Long a Letter*, Mariamma Ba points out the evils of a polygamous marriage. Ramatoulaye's husband, Modou, deserts her and marries the school mates of one of his daughters. She confesses that in her marriage "I gave freely, gave more than I received" (175). After Modou's death, his brother Tamsir is the next in line to possess her. Tamsir already has a number of wives. Ramatoulaye resists him saying, "You forget that I have a heart, a mind that I am not an object to be passed from hand to hand. You don't know what marriage means to me, it is an act of faith and love, and total surrender of myself to the person one has chosen and who has chosen you" (Sircar 175).

Several black women who were ill-treated by their husbands end up murdering them. In *Women in African Literature*, Roopali Sircar gives an analysis of such literature. She cites as instances Bessie Head's *The Collector of Treasures* and Tayeb Salih's *Migration to the North*. In the title story, "The Collection of Treasures", Dikeledi murders her husband. In prison, she finds four more women like her. She finds a bond of sisterhood with her fellow prisoners. Her husband Garego-Mokopi had left her for other woman. Years later, he had returned and claimed conjugal rights on her and accused her of having illicit relations with her dearest friend's husband, Paul. To quote from the conversation in prison with the other woman,

> "We are all here for the same crime", Kebonye said. Then with her cynical smile asked: "Do you feel any sorrow about the crime?"
> "Not really", the other woman replied.

"How did you kill him?"

"I cut off all his special parts with a knife", Dikeledi said.

"I did it with a razor", Keybonye said. She sighed and added: "I have had a troubled life" (89)

In Tayeb Salih's *Season of Migration to the North,* the heroine Bint Mahmoud, a widow was married to a lustful old man, Wad Rayyes. It was a loveless arranged marriage. The wedding night turns out to be the last night for both partners. Wad Rayyes was found dead on his marriage bed in a pool of blood with his genitals cut off. Bint Mahmoud too lay dead, having escaped from a painful life. When the eldest wife of Wad Rayyes was informed about his death she exclaims, "good riddance". She was not at all concerned and went back to sleep. She says, "Wad Rayyes dug his grave with his own hands, and Bint Mahmoud, God's blessing be upon her, paid him out in full" (128).

Female circumcision is another theme in the works of African writers. African women had to undergo several tortures to become wives and mothers. Flora Nwapa in *Efuru* and Ngugi Wa Thiong'O in *The River Between* have dealt with this theme. Female circumcision was regarded as a ritual purification which preceded the birth of a child. Feminist writers have condemned this attitude in their writings. Celebrations were conducted on the occasion of circumcision. Women submit themselves to the physical trauma. They don't make any attempt to challenge or question as it is based on the deep rooted belief that it is necessary to their womanhood. In addition to the experiences of slavery and colonialism, African women were forced to go through this hellish experience. Roopali Sircar refers to Jomo Kenyatta's defense of clitoridectomy. Kenyatta in *Facing Mount Kenya* describes it as mere bodily mutilation which is at the heart of tribal law, religion and morality and the destruction of which would destroy a whole culture. He does not recognize clitoridectomy as a way of rendering women sexually subordinate.

Several African writers have depicted the joys and pains of motherhood. Motherhood is crucial to the happiness of women. Motherhood determines womanhood. The Nigerian writers, Buchi Emecheta and Flora Nwapa have also dealt with the issues of womanhood in their novels. The title of Emecheta's novel *The Joys of Motherhood* itself is ironical. It reveals the futile purpose of a woman's life who devotes her entire life to bringing up children only to be abandoned at the end by the very same children. The protagonist Nnu Ego gave birth to nine children and in her old age she dies "a miserable death all alone like a barren woman" (219). Her situation reveals the folly of a woman who devotes her whole life for the well-being of her husband and children. She was cast out of her first husband's household because she failed to bear children. She was replaced by a younger wife in a system where polygamy provided the male with the power to marry a number of women. Her first husband Amatokwu says: "I am a busy man. I have no time to waste my precious male seed on a woman who is infertile. I have to raise children for my line. If you really want to know, you don't appeal to me anymore" (32). Nnu Ego later married Nnaife. She never liked Nnaife who did menial jobs for a white family. "She had come to him in the first place, to use him as a tool to produce the children she could not have with her first husband" (205). When her first child is dead she attempts suicide. When fate deprives her of her child, her suffering and agony is not shared by her husband. But she is able to overcome her grief and soon returns to normal life. Later she has several children. Her children do not care for their parents but they gave her a grand funeral, the second grandest in Ibuza. Many prayed to her after her death to make them fertile. But she never answered their prayers. Emecheta again discusses the concerns of motherhood in *Second Class Citizen*, an autobiographical novel. The protagonist, Adah's married life was not at all a happy one. She suffered patiently for the sake of her children. Her husband, Francis, never regarded her as his equal. She was a slave whose function was to fulfill all his needs. He was a failure who thrived on her wages. He wanted Adah to be a failure and never allowed her to rise above him. He never fulfilled his role either as a father or husband. Emecheta analyzes the strong relationship that Adah had with her children. When her son Vicky was ill, Adah asks Cynthia about her children. But Cynthia is astonished at this, because nobody had informed Adah that Vicky was ill:

> Yes, how had she known? How could a mother tell another woman who had never given birth to a baby that sometimes she lived in her children? How could she explain that if her son underwent an operation her own body would ache, how could Adah tell Cynthia that when she was looking at the fish cake, she had seen Vicky's wet face, twisting in pain, reflected in the window? There was too much to explain, too much about herself as a human being that she did not know. She just felt these things. (58)

The tragedy of barrenness is the central theme in Flora Nwapa's *Efuru*. Efuru's two husbands abandoned her and marry other women. When Efuru was sad, her mother-in-law consoles her:

> a child would come when God willed. Neighbors talked as they were bound to talk. They did not see the reason why Adizua should not marry another woman since, according to them, two men do not live together. To them Efuru was a man since she could not reproduce" (23).

She gives birth to a daughter after making several sacrifices. But the child eventually dies. After the death of her only child she returns to her father's house and dedicates her life to the selfless service of others. The novel says, "it was a curse not to have children. Her people did not just take it as one of the numerous accidents of nature. It was regarded as a failure" (207).

In Flora Nwapa's *One is Enough*, Amaka the protagonist could not produce a child in six years of married life. She begs her mother-in-law not to throw her away. Amaka achieves economic freedom and success in business. She shows that there were other ways of proving the worth of one's womanhood. Despite Amaka being an educated, loving and industrious wife, her husband prefers an illiterate imbecile to her.

An analysis of African literary texts highlights the fact that African women are not passive victims. This is also evident in the emerging works in black women's studies. Distinguished Afro-American women activists like Sojourner truth, Anna Julia Cooper, Ida Wells-Barnett and Patricia Hill Collins are supported by countless African women. The experiences that the black women suffered were entirely different from the experiences of white women. Black women form a subordinate group, which experiences a different form of reality in work, living conditions and relationships.

1

Journey towards Liberation: A Review of Black Feminist Literary Theory

The term feminism is derived from Latin 'femina' which means 'woman'. It originally meant 'having the qualities of females'. Alice Rossi has traced the first use in print to a book review published in *The Athenaeum*, 27 April 1895. The goal of feminism is to end women's subordination. It is the advocacy of women's rights based on the equality of sexes. In *Encyclopedia of Feminism* (1986), Lisa Tuttle cites Donna Hawxhurst and Sue Morrow:

> Feminism has only working definitions since it is a dynamic, constantly changing ideology with many aspects including the personal, the political and the philosophical. Feminism is a call

to action. It can never be simply a belief system. Without action, feminism is merely empty rhetoric which cancels itself out. (107)

Feminism analyses women's oppression and tries to achieve women's liberation. Charlotte Bunch (1981) has pointed out that feminism is not about 'adding in' women's rights, but about transforming society, so that feminism may be called 'transformational politics'. Lisa Tuttle also quotes Teresa Billington Grieg who opines that feminism seeks "the reorganization of the world" (108).

Mary Wollstonecraft's *A Vindication of the Rights of Woman* (1792), John Stuart Mill's *The Subjection of Women* (1869) and Margaret Fuller's *Woman in the Nineteenth Century* (1845) are some of the early noteworthy books on feminism. Feminists work for the social and cultural liberation and equality for women. In a patriarchal society, women are incapable of recognizing their creative talents. Women are regarded as 'other' in a male dominated society. The French writer Simon de Beauvoir deals with this issue in *The Second Sex* (1949) and with the prevalent myths about women in works by male writers. Male literary texts reveal a stereotypical representation of women. Such works reveal the dominance of men and the subordination of women. Several feminist critics including Kate Millet attacked the male bias in Freud's psychoanalytic theory. Male writers portray women as submissive sexual objects in their fictional works.

The male in Western civilization dominated the familial, religious, political, economic, social and artistic domains. Women are subordinated in all these domains. Women are taught to internalize assumptions on male superiority and are themselves involved in their own subordination. In *The Second Sex* Simone de Beauvouir claims, "one is not born, but rather becomes, a woman. It is civilization as a whole that produces this creature which is described as feminine" (283). In *Glossary of Literary Terms*, Abrams says that "the masculine in our culture has come to be widely identified as active, dominating, adventurous, rational, creative; the feminine, by systematic opposition to such tracts has come to be identified as passive, acquiescent, timid, emotional and conventional" (89). Many significant traditional literary works are male oriented. *Hamlet, Ulysses, Tom Jones, Oedipus Rex* are instances. Female characters are marginalized in these works. Women readers regard themselves as outsiders to these fictional works.

Judith Fetterley in *The Resisting Reader* asserts that women should make a revisionary rereading. Such a procedure will help to correct the distorted "images of women" in literary works produced by man. Men's terrors about women and their view of how a woman should behave are portrayed through their works. Women are portrayed in their literary works as docile and subservient to men's interest. Abrams says that male writers have

> managed to rise above the sexual prejudices of their time sufficiently to understand and represent the cultural pressures that have shaped the characters of women and fixed upon them their negative or subsidiary social roles; the latter class is said to include, in selected works, such authors as Chaucer, Shakespeare, Samuel Richardson, Henrik Ibsen and George Bernard Shaw. (90)

Certain feminist critics are concerned with developing a female framework for dealing with works written by women. This kind of feminist criticism is what Elaine Showalter terms gynocriticism. Literary works by gynocritics include Patricia Meyer Spacks's *The Female Imagination* (1975), Ellen Moers's *Literary Women* (1976), Elaine Showalter's *A Literature of Their Own: British Women Novelists from Bronte to Lessing* (1977) and Sandra Gilbert and Susan Gubar's *The Madwoman in the Attic* (1979). Gilbert and Gubar regard Bertha Rochester in Charlotte Bronte's *Jane Eyre* as an image of the novelist's own anxiety and rage.

Feminist critics try to discover a female literary tradition. They are also concerned with such subjects in literary works as the relationships between women, childbirth, motherhood and so on. Feminist critics also seek to find out feminist styles of language use. They have been able to unearth several female authors of the past who were silenced by male domination.

Ellen Moers in *Literary Women* (1976) states that the male writers of the nineteenth century attended universities searched for guidance or patronage and could even fight their contemporaries. But female writers of the same era were deprived of such liberties. They studied the works of other women writers and were isolated in their own homes. Moers points out the privileges and opportunities which Wordsworth and Coleridge enjoyed as men. They were university men while Jane Austen being a woman could not attend university. She had to stay in her house with her mother reading the texts of other male and female writers. Austen herself says, "I think I may boast myself to be, with all possible vanity the most unlearned and uninformed female who ever dared to be an authoress" (12). Moers states that nobody reads Mary Brunton's *Self Control* though Jane Austen was influenced by it and wrote *Sense and Sensibility* and *Mansfield Park* after reading it. Jane Austen could succeed as a writer because there was a mass of excellent, fair and wretched novels for her to study and improve upon. Moers suspects that Austen is half serious in her comment on Walter Scott:

> Walter Scott has no business to write novels, especially good ones. It is not fair – he has Fame and Profit enough as a Poet, and should not be taking the bread out of other people's mouths – I do not like him, and do not mean to like Waverley if I can help it – but fear I must. (Eagleton 13)

Feminism was viewed as a white, middle class movement and was critiqued by those who used the term 'black feminism'. This indicates that feminism is normally a movement of the whites which ignores the issues of several women who cannot be regarded either as black or white. Thus the issues of such women who cannot be treated as black or white were ignored by the white as well as the black feminists. Therefore some black feminists used the term 'womanism' and feminist critics argue for the need of feminism to include women of all race and classes.

In America, feminism arose from the Abolition movement. The Abolitionists who fought against slavery realized that though all blacks were oppressed racially, women were more oppressed because of their sex. Racial oppression took priority over sexual oppression. As bell hooks wrote in 1984, "Feminist theory would have much to offer if it showed women ways in which racism and sexism are immutably connected rather pitting one struggle against the other, or blatantly dismissing racism" (Tuttle and Hawxhurst 42).

Generally all women are oppressed. But there is a difference in the severity of oppression. Unlike white women, black women face race, class and gender oppression simultaneously. Thus black women struggle against all sorts of oppression and discard the ideas of social 'equality' prevalent in white feminism. To quote Audre Lorde, "Black feminism is not white feminism in black face" (Tuttle and Hawxhurst 42). Black women have their own issues. In *The Social Construction of Black Feminist Thought*, Patricia Hill Collins quotes Hannah Nelson: "Since I have to work, I don't really have to worry about most of the things that most of the white women I have worked for are worrying about. And if these women did their work, they would think just like I do – about this, any way" (James and Sharpley-Whiting 184-185).

Black feminism struggles against all kinds of oppression and is not limited to the issues of black women alone. In *Encyclopedia of Feminism*, Lisa Tutttle quotes the Combahee River Collective, "If black women were free, it would mean that everyone else would have to be free since our freedom would necessitate the destruction of all system of oppression" (42).

Feminist critics never got the attention they deserved. Novelists like Ekwensi and Amandi who presented a negative image of women in their novels were widely acclaimed while Buchi Emecheta and Flora Nwapa who dealt with domestic life in their works were often dismissed as limited. Male writers presented a stereotypical representation of women in their works and feminist critics point out the negative image of women portrayed in literature. "Phallocentric criticism" (Eagleton 355) excluded women authored fictions.

Though male writers like Chinua Achebe and James Ngugi have succeeded in making their presence felt, many first-rate black women writers are still unheard of. The portrayal of women in their fictional works is based on their real life experiences and women are shown as wives, mothers, daughters, traders and revolutionaries.

Roopali Sircar in *The Twice Colonized: Women in African Literature* asserts that Wilfred Cartey's *Whispers from a Continent* (1969) is the first work to identify female presence in African literature. E.M. Obiechina's *Culture, Tradition and Society and the West African novel* (1975) provide a short discussion of women's lives in the context of culture. These books are written by men and so provide a male point of view. There is an overwhelming male bias in the portrayal of women in these works. G.C.M. Mutiso's essay, "Women in African Literature" and Kenneth Little's *The Sociology of Urban Women's Image in African Literature* give detailed analysis of African women in literature but, again, both are marred by male bias. In "The Social Construction of Black Feminist Thought", Patricia Hill Collins refers to Ruth Shays' claim that the difference in experiences of men and women lead to difference in perspective: "The mind of the man and the mind of the woman is the same. But this business of living makes women use their minds in ways that men don't even have to think about" (James and Sharpley-Whiting 185). Many women writers like Marion Kilsan in "Women and African Literature", Rosean P. Bell in "The Absence of the African Woman Writer" and Yinka Shoga in "Women Writers and African Literature" have succeeded in portraying female experience with authenticity. African male writers like Ngugi Wa Thiong O' and Sembene Ousmane were concerned with women's issues and challenged patriarchal society. These male writers too can be termed as feminists.

For more than two centuries, Afro-American women have struggled against the oppression of race, economy, gender and class. Afro-American feminism was shaped by the experience of the slaves and later by legal and political discrimination against 'free' people of African descent. They struggled against racism, sexism, sexual violence and poverty. But the struggles of black women have been obscured by the feminist practices of white women and the sexism prevalent in patriarchal society.

All black feminists in America are marginalized and they are outsiders in American culture. But their response to this marginalization is sometimes mistaken for an intrinsic radicalism. Black feminism is especially complex because of ideological differences among black feminists. Though diverse in outlook, black feminism is characterized by common concerns for racial and gender equality. Several intellectuals are active supporters of black feminism.

Early activists of black feminism include Sojourner Truth, Maria Stewart and Harriet Tubman in the antebellum era; Anna Julia Cooper and Ida B. Wells in the post Reconstruction age; Amy Jacques Garvey of the United Negro Improvement Association, Zora Neale Hurston of the Harlem Renaissance, and Fannie Lou Hamer, Ella Baker and Lorraine Hansberry of the civil rights era. Several other black women writers and intellectuals also have made significant contributions to the struggle.

Sojourner truth is one of the best known black feminist activists of the antebellum era. Her speeches – "Women's Rights" and "When Woman Gets Her Right Man will be Right" are of special significance. She declared, "Ain't I a woman?" at the Women's Rights Conference held in 1851 at Aleron, Ohio. When she started to speak white women wanted her to be silenced. She was finally permitted to speak and she spoke about the impact of slavery on black women.

> Look at my arm! I have ploughed and planted and gathered into barns, no man could head me – and ain't I a woman? I could work as much and eat as much as a man – when I could get it and bear the lash as well! And ain't I a woman? I have borne thirteen children, and seen most of 'em sold into slavery, and when I cried out with my mother's grief, none but Jesus heard me – and ain't I a woman? (James and Sharply-Whiting 220)

Maria W. Stewart is a free black Bostonian who was one of the first US women political speakers. She was branded a heretic and was excommunicated from church and prevented from speaking in public by African-American clergyman. She later served in the medical corps during the American Civil War.

Harriet Tubman, a contemporary of Stewart, was the first American woman to lead black and white troops in battle. She won the people's title of 'General Tubman'. She fought as a soldier and escaped slavery. She led thousands of people to freedom through the Underground Railroad before freedom. Anna Julia Cooper and Ida B. Wells chronicled their experiences in their memoirs *A Voice from the South: By a Black Woman of the South* (1892) and *Crusade for Justice: The Autobiography of Ida B. Wells* (1970).

In the civil rights and Black Liberation movements of the 1950s, 1960s and the early 1970s many black women worked in organizations that aimed to uplift black women. Such organizations include Southern

Christian Leadership Council (SCLC), The Student Nonviolent Coordinating Committee (SNCC), the Congress on Racial Equality (CORE), the organization of Afro-American Unity (OAAU) and the Black Panther Party (BPP). These political organizations worked for the development of women. In the 1950s Ella Baker attained the position of a leader in SCLC, an organization led by Reverend Martin Luther King Jr. This alienated many male members of the organization. These organizations created new progressive gender roles but did not use the term feminism. Third World Women's Alliance grew out of SNCC. In the seventies women activists like Angela Davis, Toni Cade Bambara, Audre Lorde, Sonia Sanchez, Alice Walker and Ntozake Shange criticized capitalism and racism in their writings and speeches.

During the movement era from 1955 to 1975 male intellectuals like Franz fanon, Amilicar Cabral and Malcolm X influenced many black women. The term 'feminist' then denoted exclusively the experience of white women. So these black feminist regarded themselves as 'antiracists'. By the 1980s, black women struggles came to be grouped under 'feminism'. Antiracist feminism is relevant to all progressive women and is different from black feminism or 'womanism'. Afro-American women's gender-based progressive activism was still without any specific or distinctive name.

In *International Encyclopaedia of Women,* Joy James cites Alice Walker who introduced the term 'womanism' to contrast black feminism with white Western feminism. Walker states, "For white women there is apparently no felt need to preface 'feminist' with the word 'white' since the word 'feminist' is accepted as coming out of white women culture" (710). In the view of Patricia Hill Collins,

> the term black feminist both highlights the contradictions
> underlying the assumed Whiteness of feminism and reminds
> White women that they are neither the only nor the normative

'feminists'. Because it challenges black women to confront their own views on sexism and women's oppression, the term Black feminism also makes many African American women uncomfortable. (710)

Black lesbians like Audre Lorde and Barbara Smith have made significant contributions to black feminism. There have been many recent developments in womanist ideology and black male feminists have also made significant contributions.

In *International Encyclopedia of Women – Global Women's Issues and Knowledge* Vol. 1, Joy James points out that the infant mortality rate of Afro-American women is twice that of their white counterparts. Poverty rates are also higher than that of the general population. Contemporary black feminists deal with issues like sexual/racial violence, and child welfare, and advocate the human rights of prisoners. Studies prove that by June 1997, 138000 women were imprisoned in the United States and this is ten times the number of women imprisoned in Spain, England, France, Scotland, Germany and Italy put together. African-American feminism had a wide impact and this activism could influence women belonging to other cultures.

Alice Walker suggests two reasons for the oppression of black women writers in America:

There are two reasons why the black woman writer is not taken as seriously as the black male writer. One is that she is a woman. Critics seem unusually ill-equipped to intelligently discuss and analyse the works of black women. Generally, they do not even make the attempt; they prefer, rather, to talk about the lives of black women writers, not about what they write. And, since black women writers are not – it would seem – very likeable – until recently they were the least willing worshippers of male supremacy – comments about them tend to be cruel. (O' Brien 201)

"Black British feminism" denotes the theory and practice of feminism among the black women in Britain. Black feminism is related to the black women's movement in the 1970s. Black women's concerns were marginalized by the white feminist movement as well as by anti-racist movements. Black women established organizations such as Brixton Black Women's Group, Liverpool Black Sisters and Awaz to deal with the issues that concerned them.

Though the term black feminism came in use in the 1970s, there were many Black feminist workers like Cornelia Sorabji, Amy Garvey and Claudia Jones before the 70s. They focused on issues of race, class and gender. Cornelia Sorabji was the first woman law student in a British university. She came to India in 1894 and fought for women in purdah. Amy Garvey was the leader of association for the advancement of Coloured People. Claudia Jones came to Britain in 1956 and established the Confederation of Afro-Asian-Caribbean organizations. Black women played active roles in anti-imperialist and anti-racist struggles. These organizations include the Indian Home Rule Movement, the League of Colored People, and the Campaign against Racism and Discrimination (CARD).

In 1978, the organization of Women of African and Asian Descent (OWAAD) came into being. Its important campaigns during 1978-82 were for immigration legislation and against domestic violence, school exclusions, deportation cases and the busing of school children. OWAAD protested against the Immigration and Nationality Act of 1981, which sort to withdraw the right to abode of many passport holders from former British Colonies and reinforced the position of women immigrants as dependents. Internal divisions caused the end of OWAAD. But campaigns were led by organizations like Southall Black Sisters. Black feminist theory emerged from the black women's movement. It challenged the white feminist theory that ignored black women's struggle. Black women created a theory based on black women's experiences of oppression and resistance.

According to Carby, black women's experiences challenged that of white feminists in the areas of family, reproduction and patriarchy. For black women the family was a site of resistance against racism. Unlike white women, black women were not valued as child-rearers and homemakers. Carby claimed that white feminists' reliance on the notion of global patriarchal dominance by men over women marked the intersection of race with gender. By the late 1980s black feminists became more concerned with the issues of internal difference and heterogeneity. Contemporary black feminist theory acknowledges black women's multiple, hybrid and complex realities.

Women can attain their full potential with the help of education. According to some feminists educational achievement is related to personal development and success. Others claim that educational achievement has an important role in the welfare of family and society. Women are prevented from achieving success in education due to issues of race, class and gender. Females may not be enrolled in school or may fail to complete a stage of their education and maybe a 'minority' in educational institutions. These are some of the issues that affect the educational progress of women.

The educational achievement of black women is affected by discrimination based on race, class and gender. Exploitation, poverty, marginalization and denial of rights and privileges are their common experiences. They display an ambivalent attitude towards educational achievement. Educational success involves identification with the dominant culture and separation from their own culture. Educational achievement is also a way of resistance to the dominant culture and gives women a sense of personal control.

Black feminists have been skeptical about the role of education in overturning or transforming social inequalities. Legislation has an even greater role than education in preventing racial and sexual discrimination. Black intellectuals have pointed out the need to represent the black and minority cultures within the curriculum. Black feminist have also pointed out that gender issues are more prominent in the curriculum than issues of race.

Virginia Woolf says in *A Room of One's Own* that masterpieces are not single and solitary births; they are the outcome of many years of thinking in common, of thinking by the body of the people, so that the experience of the mass is behind the single voice" (Eagleton 10). This points to the need for a literary tradition and is applicable to the works of black women too. Black feminist critics try to discover a tradition of women writers silenced by centuries of oppression. They tried to provide a context that would support contemporary women writers and reveal the perceptions of these unknown writers. Their works have led to the expansion of black feminist literary criticism and the establishment of feminist publishing houses. Earlier these writers were excluded from courses in universities and schools. Now leaders have become aware of such new areas of women's writings.

Being a black literate woman was a punishable crime in America. Black women had ancestors with creative talents. Some were able to keep alive the creative spark they had inherited. Black women did not have the freedom to paint, to sculpt, to read or to write. Alice Walker states in the title essay in *In Search of Our Mother's Gardens* that there were many women with real gifts who could have been great writers but for the suppression of their talent. She also refers to Phyllis Wheatley, a slave of the 1700s. Walker claims that if she had been white she might have been considered the intellectual superior of all women and most of the men of her day.

Alice Walker quotes Virginia Woolf's well-known statement that a woman writer of fiction needs "a room of her own (with a key and lock) and enough money to support herself" (Eagleton 34). Walker was captured at seven and enslaved. She was burdened by her need to express herself and suffered from poor health, malnutrition and mental agonies. Despite all this, she was forced to do strenuous work to feed her small children and eventually she died.

Black women writers use their own experiences as well as the experiences of their predecessors in their literary creations. Black feminist critics want the black female writer to know and assimilate the experiences of earlier black women writers. But such works are out of print, abandoned, discredited or lost. Alice Walker in "Saving the life that is your own: The Importance of Models in the Artist's Life" asserts a black woman writer should make use of the experiences of her predecessors.

Walker wrote a story "The Revenge of Hannah Kemhuff," based on the experiences of her own mother and Zora Neale Hurston's folklore collection of the 1920s. It was selected as one of the best short stories of 1974. The literary creations of these women writers are authentic as they are derived from their own experiences. Walker's mother was humiliated by a white woman when she went to apply for some government surplus food at a local commissary. Later her mother witnessed the same white women grow old and senile and so badly crippled that she couldn't walk without two sticks. Walker states:

> In that story I gathered up the historical and psychological threads of the life my ancestors lived, and in writing of it I felt joy and strength and my own continuity. I had that wonderful feeling writers get sometimes, not very often, of being 'with' a great many people, ancient spirits, all very happy to see me consulting and acknowledging them, and eager to let me know, through the joy of their presence, that indeed, I am not alone. (Eagleton 32-33)

In the 1970s Afro-American women were able to make public their search for themselves in literary culture. In "But What Do We

Think We're Doing, Anyway", Barbara Christian states that the featuring of Zora Neale Hurston in the most widely read publication of Afro-American literature, *Black World* in August 1974 pointed to the shift in interest among the readers about women's creativity. Several essays on Hurston were also published in that issue. There are many significant black fiction writers like Maya Angelou, Toni Cade Bambara, Paule Marshall, Toni Morrison and Alice Walker. Their existence pointed to their unknown literary predecessors who had prepared the way for them. The great works of contemporary blacks would not have been possible otherwise. Zora Neale Hurston is one such neglected literary foremother. But she has been recognized by her daughters and is now regarded as a major figure in the Afro-American literary tradition.

Black women writers are soon forgotten and this is one of the reasons why they do not have a tradition. They are discovered 'accidentally'. Though Paul Marshall's *Brown Girl, Brownstones* was published in 1959 and Hurston's Their *Eyes were Watching God* in 1937 they were unknown even in the eighties. Black male writers were more privileged because their works reappeared in the sixties. Even significant women writers like Bambara, Jordan, Morrison, Walker and Shirley Anne Williams were ignored by the critics. Christian states in "But What Do We Think We're Doing Anyway" that she found it impossible to locate the works of many nineteenth century and contemporary writers because such books went in and out of print like ping-pong balls. She says, "At times I felt more like a detective than a literary critic as I chased clues to find a book I knew existed but which I had begun to think I had hallucinated" (42). Black writers should turn to black tradition and develop a theory of their own.

In the 'The Laugh of Medusa' Helen Cixous claims that women inhabit a pre-civilizational world, which is closer to nature and comparable to Black Africa: "they can be thought that their territory is black;

because you are Africa, you are black. Your continent is dark. Dark is dangerous" (333). Kadiatu Kanneh also quotes Helen Cixous in "Love, Mourning and Metaphor: Terms of Identity", "We the precocious, we the repressed of culture, our lovely mouths gagged with pollen, our wind knocked out of us, we the labyrinths, the ladders, the trampled spaces, the bevies ... We are black and we are beautiful (333).

Critics like Ngugi Wa Thiong O' are of the view that Western colonial powers refer to African people in ways that emphasize the position of women outside history and culture. This could be seen as part of their purpose to wipe out the achievements and the traditions of the colonized.

Barbara Smith in "Towards a Black Feminist Criticism" cites Jerry H. Bryant, a white male reviewer who says that there is "nothing feminist" about Alice Walker's "In Love and Trouble: Stories of Black Women" (Eagleton 123). He considers blackness and feminism mutually exclusive. Robert Bone, another white critic, in *The Negro Novel in America* dismisses Ann Petry's classic *The Street* as "a superficial social analysis" (180). Sara Blackburn in a review of Toni Morrison's *Sula* recognizes Morrison as a gifted writer but criticizes her for dealing with Black folk, particularly the double non-entities, black women. In Blackburn's view in order to be accepted as 'serious', 'important', 'talented' and 'American' Morrison should refocus her writings:

> Toni Morrison is far too talented to remain only a marvelous recorder of the black side of provincial American life. If she is to maintain the large and serious audience she deserves she is going to have to address a riskier contemporary reality than this beautiful but nevertheless distanced novel. (Eagleton 123)

This reveals the racist flaw in black literary criticism. Several western critics who were able to unearth dozens of obscure white women writers remain ignorant about black women writers. Black feminist critics like Smith argue that white women should include black women writers in their research and writing. Black women were not able to make the progress that white women made because of their colour, economic power and the strength and support of a movement. One of the major tasks of black feminist criticism is to create a climate in which black writers can survive.

The early supporters of feminist literary criticism were white females who regarded the experience of white middle class women as the norm. They excluded the works of black women writers from literary anthologies and critical studies. Deborah E. Mc Dowell in her essay "New Directions for Black Feminist Criticism" cites Patricia Meyer Spacks who in her *The Female Imagination* focused on women in the Anglo-American literary tradition. Spacks defensively quotes Philips Chesler, a white female psychologist, "As a white woman I'm reluctant and unable to construct theories about experiences I haven't had" (5). To this, Alice Walker retorts, "Spacks never lived in nineteenth century Yorkshire, so why theorize about the Brontës?" (50)

Several black critics point out that, white women should recognize the black women in their writing. Mc Dowell in "New Directions for Black Feminist Criticism" cites Andrea Benton's claim that white women's categorization of women is Euro-American and hence they cannot take into account black women characters.

In the seventies most feminist journals were white publications and dealt exclusively with white women as if they were the only women in the United States. Barbara Smith believed that black women writers were excluded by white feminist literature because "a parallel black feminist movement had been slower in evolving" (Eagleton 123). Feminist theorists do not take into account the fact that women are of many races and ethnic background and different histories and cultures. If these facts were to be taken into account, their articulation of a theory would be less facile. They fail to acknowledge the existence of black women and the theory they invent has therefore no relevance to black women.

Even in the field of literature, black people experience a kind of slavery worse than physical bondage. The white westerners subjugated black writers. These writers were dependent on the white Western tradition. Henry Louis Gates, Jr., in "Writing Race and the Difference it Makes", cites the instance of Edmond Laforest, a member of the Haitian literary movement called La Ronde, who tied a Larousse Dictionary around his neck and drowned himself. Quoting Jacques Derrida, Louis says black people should learn to speak the other's language without pronouncing (our) own (Eagleton 46). Literature is related to race. Black literature reflects racial difference. Western critical theory should not be adopted in the analysis of the works of black writers. Black theorists have already begun their efforts to discover a black literary tradition.

Bell hooks in "Black Women: Shaping Feminist Theory" quotes Leah Fritz:

> Women's suffering under sexist tyranny is a common bond among all women, transcending the particulars of the different forms that tyranny takes. *Suffering cannot be measured and compared quantitatively.* Is the enforced idleness and vacuity of a 'rich' woman, which leads her to madness and or suicide, greater or less than suffering of a poor woman who barely survives on welfare but retains somehow her spirits? There is no way to measure such difference, but should these two women survey each other without the screen of patriarchal class status, they may find a commonality in the fact that they are both oppressed, both miserable. (James and Sharpley-Whiting 134)

Here there is a conscious effort on the part of a white woman to equate the suffering of the white women and black women. The lifestyle of a white female is different from that of her black counterpart. White women are definitely more privileged than black women and the suffering of black women who are subjugated by black men, white men and white women is more intense than that of white women.

Bell hooks accuses Betty Friedan of ignoring black women in *Feminine Mystique* which paved the way for the feminist movement. White feminists ignored the black writers who were powerless to change their condition in life and suffered mentally, physically and spiritually. Racism in American Society led to class struggle. The writings of white feminist reflect racism. Early feminists ignored the link between race and class.

All women suffer the oppression of gender. Bell hooks states that under capitalism patriarchy is so structured that women are restricted in some realms and unlimited freedom is allowed in other realms. Thus women ignore their discrimination and even imagine that they are not oppressed at all.

Though there are a number of books on feminism very few deal with the issues of race and racism. They mostly deal with the relationship between and black and white. Sexism is a form of oppression similar to racism. Both are identity-based forms of oppression that subjugate a group of people deemed unfit for self-governance. They are paid little or nothing for their work because such work constitutes their natural lot. 'White supremacy' and 'male supremacy' legitimized social hierarchies and corresponded to oppression based on race and sex respectively.

Some feminists give priority to sexism. Early radical feminists made sexism significant by portraying racism as an extension of sexism. According to them sexism served as a model for other forms of social hierarchy. Linda Martin Alcoff in "Racism" cites Mary Daly's claim that racism is a patriarchal way of creating divisions among women. Margaret A. Simons opposed this view.

White women seldom play a significant role in black women's Liberation. Adrienne Rich speaks of 'white solipsism' in this context. Rich regards sexism as more significant than racism. She portrays white women as victims of racism and not as agents who promote it. She feels that some white women were interested in making alliances with other women.

The social status of privileged bourgeois women is different from that of the mass of women. Middle class women enjoy more freedom than working class women. They have access to universities, publishing houses, mass media and money. They are isolated from black women and their concerns are different from theirs. If black women had spoken of their oppression, they would have been attacked from all sides. Working class black women experienced varying degrees of patriarchal tyranny and they devised strategies of their own to resist male dominance. Black women know that they were oppressed but they could not articulate a written theory like the white women.

In "Black Women: Shaping Feminist Theory", bell hooks says:

When I participated in feminist groups I found that white women adopted a condescending attitude towards me and other non-white participants. The condescension they directed at black women was one of the means they employed to remind us that the women's movement was 'theirs' – that we were able to participate because they allowed it, men encouraged it; afterall, we were needed to legitimate the process. They did not see us as equals. They did not treat us as equals. And though they expected us to provide firsthand accounts of black experience, they felt it was their role to decide if these experiences were authentic. (Eagleton 141)

White women never acknowledge their subjugation of black women but instead they project themselves as powerless, passive victims. Western feminists focus on class and gender and do not consider race as a crucial factor. Black men, though oppressed by racism are privileged by virtue of their gender. They in turn act as oppressors and exploiters of black women. White women act as oppressors and exploiters of black people.

Angela Davis provides accounts of sexist racism. Racial discrimination is manifest even in the works of some white feminists. Black men who violated the chastity of 'pure' white women were tortured and even burnt to death. Davis states that some white feminists perpetuated the myth that black men are especially prone to commit rape.

Feminists should try to resolve the differences among women because underemphasizing such differences can cause alienation and distrust among black women. Some feminist critics like Ann Ferguson and Allison Jaggar argued for socialist feminism. There has been a long tradition of African women's struggle for freedom and black feminists point out that feminism is not a western invention. Women have generally been silenced but the pressure behind the silence has been greater in the case of black women.

Western writers characterized African women as timid, passive and family oriented. They are the victims of the worst type of male chauvinism. Western women are seen to be more knowledgeable and dynamic. They have fought against similar oppression and won social, economic and political liberation of a kind. Western ideology failed to recognize the heterogeneity of pre-colonial African societies. They assumed that male chauvinism is similar in all human societies and they failed to recognize the fine picture of male-female relationships in Africa.

The Western view about human nature is found in religion, history, literature and science. In the religious context, woman is said to have brought woe and suffering to humanity. In literature, women were regarded as insignificant both as readers and producers of text. In science, a woman is seen as less intelligent and as belonging to the weaker sex. There are not many books that reveal African views on women and this is a major concern in the development of African feminist philosophy.

Though there are few authentic texts on traditional African beliefs and thoughts, the highly developed oral tradition reveals many of their beliefs and views. African feminist philosophers and feminist critics and writers make use of this to reveal that women enjoyed a better status in traditional African societies. Women dominated the economic, social and political spheres of life in traditional African societies. In traditional society there were greater opportunities for self-development for women. Sophie Oluwele in "Africa" refers to Bolanle Awe who claims that African women were economically disempowered and politically disenfranchised during the colonial era.

Another prevailing view is that though there were a few successful women, the majority of them were oppressed. Black feminists should be aware of the basic ideas, beliefs and principles upon which African society is based if they want to see a change in the present subordinate position of women. Though African men could never consider women their equals, they acknowledged the positive traits in women.

Black women artists survived the harshness of life and emerged with principled dignity. Their strength, courage and refusal to accept domination form the essence of their creative achievements. They were prohibited by law and traditional customs to participate in creative endeavors. They were treated as manual laborers without intelligence and were regarded as objects of sexual pleasure. In spite of all the oppression they invented their own unique form of aesthetic expression. Their life stories are not just tales of stoic endurance or mute acceptance. Black women's narrative reveals their ability to withstand and oppose repressive circumstances.

The literary scholar Barbara Christian was one of the first to trace a history of black women writers dating back to the nineteenth century. Her initial efforts led to a fruitful discovery of the responsibility of black feminist critics. Black women pursued their creative impulses in the face of imposed constraints and produced objects of lasting value. Alice Walker in "In Search of Our Mother's Gardens" speaks of the psychic toll on black women who do not find an outlet for their talents. According to Walker they are "driven to a numb and bleeding madness by the springs of creativity in them for which there is no release" (34). Black women's creativity was kept alive when they made art a part of their daily lives - in their gardens, quilts, sculptures, pottery, sewing and so on.

Black women's existence, experiences, culture and their subjugation were invisible to the white community. Though a large body of work has been published on the subject of women's writings, very few of these were by black women or by women in post-colonial societies in the seventies. Black women wanted their experiences to be published and felt profound pain in the absence of such works. Black women's writing can be properly understood only from a black feminist critical perspective. As Barbara Smith says in her landmark essay, "I think of the thousands and thousands of books which have been devoted by this time to the subject of women's writing and I am filled with rage at the fraction of these pages that mention black and other third world women" (41).

Black male writers like Darwin Turner and Ishmael Reed openly attacked black women writers. Darwin Turner in *In a Minor Chord: Three Afro-American writers and their Search for Identity* states that the black woman writer Zora Neale Hurston is "artful", "coy", "irrational", "superficial" and "shallow" (125). The denunciation of black women by black men is in perfect agreement with the values of the society. In "Toward a Black Feminist Criticism", Smith quotes Ora Williams who points out the reactions of her colleagues toward her efforts to research black women writers. Others too have reacted negatively with such statements as, "I really don't think you are going to find very much written", "Have they written anything that is good?" And "I wouldn't go overboard with the women's lib thing" (Eagleton 126). In *The Negro Novel in America,* Robert Bone analyses Jessie Fauset's novels and says that Fauset's novels remain obscure because the emphasis is on the black middle class and this results in novels that are uniformly sophomoric, trivial and dull" (Eagleton 101). The literature of black women was regarded as an 'insignificant', 'nonexistent' body of literature. Alice Walker in "Saving the life that is your own" refers to Puchett who wonders in the "The Negro and his Folkways and Superstitions" "if 'The Negro' had a large enough brain" (Eagleton 31).

Black women's writings were excluded from schools and universities. ATCAL (Association for the Teaching of Caribbean and African and Asian Literature) was formed to change the prevailing attitudes. It aimed "to convince the examining bodies to accord examination status to this literature, for it is essential for the young of whatever race to understand Black experience" (Eagleton) 129.

The whites regard black literature as minority literature. Toni Morrison cites one of the reasons for the general ignorance of black writers. Blacks were seen as discredited people and their creations were also discredited. Black writers were excluded from the academic circles. Barbara Christian assets in "The Race for Theory" that "many of our literatures (certainly Afro-American literature) are central, not minor (Eagleton 277)

The writings of black women are not part of mainstream writing. The black cultural resurgence of the 1960s and the 1970s shows the necessity of critical writing by persons outside the 'mainstream'. Black literature was regarded as a subcategory of mainstream literature due to racism. Black women's works contain a stunningly accurate record of the impact of patriarchal values and practices upon the lives of women and provides an insight into female experience.

Borrowing the assumptions of Kolodny, Deborah E. Mc Dowell in "New Directions for Black Feminist Criticism" gives a vague definition of black feminist criticism:

> Black feminist critics analyse the works of black female writers from a feminist or political perspective. But the term can also apply to any criticism written by a Black woman regardless of her subject or perspective - a book written by a male from a feminist or political perspective, a book written by a black woman or about Black women authors in general, or any writings by women. (Eagleton 230)

Black feminist critics should draw on the scholarship of feminists in other disciplines. Feminist theory ought to be strengthened and feminist critics should take into consideration the deformation implicit in the theory. Some women have a more privileged position than others. The relations of power between women should also be made visible. Women in general are silenced but some are more silenced than others.

There are several commonalities in the texts of black women writers. Mc Dowell points out several similarities in her essay. The theme of the thwarted female artist is prominent in the works of Alice Walker and Toni Morrison. Pauline Breedlove in Morrison's *The Bluest Eyes* is obsessed with putting things in order. Similarly, Eva Peace in Morrison's *Sula* is forever rearranging the pleats in her dress. The imagery of color is central to the writings of black women writers. In Jessie Fauset's short story *The Sleeper Wakes*, Amy who is blinded by fairy tale notions of love and marriage, wears pink, which suggests innocence and immaturity. After her marriage Amy no longer wears pink. In Hurston's Their *Eyes were Watching God*, Janie's apron, her silks and satins, her head scarves all symbolized various stages of her journey from captivity to liberation. The motif of journey recurs in the works of black women writers. Black women writers use the motif in a way that is different from that of their male counterparts. For black men a journey means a decent into the underworld as in the case of Ralph Ellison's *Invisible Man* and Richard Wright's "The Man who lived Underworld". The black female's journey is basically personal and psychological journey. The female characters move from "victimization to consciousness" as Mc Dowell has noted (Eagleton 233). Black feminist critics should explore how such commonalities are manifested differently in black women's writing and the ways in which these are depicted by black male writers.

In "Writing 'Race' and the Difference it Makes" Henry Louis Gates, Jr. cites Rebecca Cox Jackson, a black visionary who claims that God appeared to her in her dream as a white man and taught her the word of God. Alice Walker's revision of this, points out the need of black women to have a theory of their own. The dialogue between Celie and Shug in *The Color Purple* asserts the need to turn away from 'the old white man' and mentions the need to eliminate 'man' as a mediator between woman and 'everything'.

"You have to git man off your eyeball, before you can see anything a'all."

"Man corrupts everything", says Shug. "He on your box of grits, in your head, and all over the radio. He try to make you think he everywhere. Soon after you think he everywhere, you think be God. But he ain't whenever you trying to pray, a man plop himself on the other end of it, tell him to get lost, say Shug (179).

As Toril Moi observes, the main theoretical task for male feminists is to develop "an analysis of their own position, and a strategy for how their awareness of their difficult and contradictory position in relation to feminism can be made explicit in discourse and practice" (James and Sharpley-Whiting 88).

From ancient times Africa has exerted a powerful hold on the Western imagination. Often writings by Europeans about Africa, paintings, literature and travelogues created during European exploration in the seventeenth, eighteenth and nineteenth centuries provide distorted images of Africa. The British, the French, the Dutch and the Portuguese had different experiences in Africa. Europeans viewed Africans as distinct from them. The European imagination exaggerated the differences between themselves and the Africans and assumed that the behaviour of Africans was unnatural.

International Encyclopaedia of Women notes that Europeans personified the African continent as "an irresistible destructive woman luring male European slavers, explorers and settlers and ultimately destroying them". In European fiction "Africa is symbolized as a woman, as a fecund womb to be exploited and controlled" (1101). Black women were seen as less 'womanly' than their European counterparts. They were not considered whole individuals with intellect and body. They were regarded as menial workers and as sexual objects to satisfy men's primal urges. European writers who had little contact with African women and who had little knowledge of African women's social roles, popularized through literature and art, images which devalue African women. Westerners learned about women in Africa through novels, memoirs, religious tracts and art. As in the past we do not see, hear or learn much about the lives of African women in the present.

News, particularly television news programmes portray women as secondary. Here the unequal power relation in a patriarchal society is dominan. Africa remains the 'dark continent' of Joseph Conrad's *Heart of Darkness* (1902). Africa is viewed as a 'distant', 'alien' place where 'exotic' people live. News media often do not provide adequate coverage to Africa, for various reasons. African women, their voices and their activities are often neglected. Women in Africa are more invisible than men in Africa. In American news stories black women are insignificant as acting or speaking sources. The predominant image of black women found on American television was that of them weeping. Women were the voiceless symbols of male brutality. Men are more frequently heard and seen on television. The stereotypical portraiture of Afro-American women in literary works and films is based on race, class and gender discrimination.

Authentic portrayal of African women's lives reveals them to be inspirational. It also exposes the endurance of women confronted by political, economic and social challenges. Popular media have trivialized, marginalized, victimized or ridiculed African women. They were not authentically portrayed. Even media stories targeting a female audience treat women stereotypically. Women of color were underrepresented in feminist literature and this reveals the reality of racism within the women's movement. Black women and other oppressed groups cannot expect themselves to be represented in popular culture. They are symbolically annihilated.

Though often members of a patriarchal society, African women enjoy economic independence in varying degrees. Married women usually have a separate income distinct from that of their husbands and have the right to acquire property. In some regions, men and women have equal rights to use land. Women who acquired Western education turned to professions like teaching, clerical work, nursing and midwifery. Others tried to get work in cooking, manufacturing goods, or turned to agriculture. In addition to other occupations most women were engaged in trading. Evidence shows that even in the pre-colonial past women engaged in trade. Economic independence of women is a necessity in most African societies such as Igbo or the Ga of Ghana. Working women had more independence and more control over the products of their labour.

Roopali Sircar says that in the colonial period, women were excluded from cash crop cultivation. Men were taught modern techniques to raise the level of production. As a result women's labor came to be viewed as inferior. When man worked in distant place women had to support themselves and their children. The migrant men's wages were usually very low. Women earned what they could through trade and agriculture.

The publishing industry has ignored and silenced the views and ideas of black women. The exclusion of the views of black women by the publishing industry reflects the racism and sexism of society. Black women's voices are often unheard. Works by and about black women were totally ignored even in the eighties. Attempts were made by feminist publishers to make the voices of black women heard.

'Black Woman Talk' is a collective of women of Asian and African descent living in Britain. Black Woman Talk began as a small group of unemployed women who formed a workers publishing cooperative. Black women's work expresses their experience and history. Black Woman Talk provided a means by which women of Asian and African descent could publish their work. The experiences revealed in the writings of black women help the wider community to understand the lives and history of black women. Works produced by black women should be available for use in schools, libraries and other public information centres. Black Woman Talk is an example of the attempts made by black women to create their own means of communication.

Until recently white males dominated most publishing houses. The situation has slightly changed and prestigious publishing houses like Virago, The Women's Press and Zed press have started to publish the works of black women. Jessica Huntley founded Bogle-L'Ouverture Publications, one of the oldest companies to publish the writings of black women. Buchi Emecheta also started her own company. In 1987, Iyamide Hazeley and Adeola Solanke established Zora Press, a women's publishing house. New Beacon Books, Karnak House, Akira and Karia are other black publishers.

Deborah Mc Dowell in "New Directions of Black Feminist Criticism" quotes William Morgan who claims that the writings of women have been "patronized, slighted and misunderstood by a cultural establishment operating according to male norms out of male perceptions (24). The literature of black women is the direct result of their shared political, social and economic experience. There are innumerable commonalities in works by black women, including the use of black women's language. Black feminist criticism embodies the spirit of black women's art and asserts the connections between the work and the political situation of all black women. Black feminist criticism is the result of a black feminist movement and it can contribute ideas that the movement could use.

Black male writers too ignored the works of black women writers. Deborah McDowell in "New Directions for Black Feminist Criticism" states that black women are conspicuously absent from the table of contents in Robert Stepto's *From behind the veil: A study of Afro-American Narrative.* Though he gives a two-page discussion of Zora Neale Hurston's *Their Eyes were Watching God,* he did not feel the novel merited a chapter or thorough analysis. But he acknowledges it to be a "seminal narrative in Afro-American letters" (25). McDowell cites David Littlejohn who praises post 1940 black fiction, but is hostile to the works of Fauset and Nella Larsen. He praises black fiction because "the newer writers are obviously writing as men, for men" (25). Mary Ellman refers to this type of criticism as 'phallic criticism', criticism that is based on male-centered values and definitions.

White women, white men and black men consider their experiences as normative and black women's experiences as deviant. Black feminist critics are now engaged in the task of unearthing forgotten black women writers and revising misinformed views about them. Mc Dowell in her essay explores the limitations of black feminist scholarship. Black feminist scholarship is more practical than theoretical. The theories lack sophistication and are damaged by slogans, rhetoric and idealism. The articles based on these theories often lack precision and detail. Mc Dowell points out that, black feminist critics must have a thorough knowledge of black literature and black culture in general.

Barbara Christian says that while writing *Black Women Novelists: The Development of a Tradition* (1980) she searched for a full length work on Afro American women's history. The only one she could find was Gerda Lerner's *Black Women in White America* (1973). She found only a few paragraphs devoted to women in most of the other books. It was only after she had completed her work that Sharon Harley and Rosalyn Terbog Penn's historical essays *The Afro- American Woman* (1978) was published. Even in 1978, a full-length study of black women writers was not available though in the 1970s black women published more novels than they had in any other decade. A black feminist political theory is necessary because white males, black males and white females who had access to critical publications did not 'know' how to respond to the works of black women. Black women were the only ones who were interested in the writings of black women authors. Christian claims that black women who belongs to the lower strata of the society read black women's novels with "unheard intensity" (43- 44). They often begged or 'borrowed' books and the sales figures do not necessary reflect their interest.

African literature is as significant as any other literature. Henry Louis Gates, Jr. in the *Introduction to Writing 'Race' and the Difference it Makes,* quotes Anthony Appiah who claims that we must not ask "the reader to understand Africa by embedding it in European culture" (Eagleton 48). Black women's existence, experience and culture and their subjugation were invisible to the white community and male consciousness. Feminists in general were blind to the implications of any womanhood other than white womanhood and this ignorance was based on deep racism.

McDowell in "New Directions of Black Feminist Criticism" speaks of a contextual approach, which appeals for a study of black literature based on black history and culture. But this is often dismissed by critics who insist on textual and linguistic analysis. Mc Dowell favours the 'contextual' approach because it reveals the conditions under which literature is produced, published and reviewed. She insists that black feminist critics should be aware of the significance of both the contextual approach and that of textual and linguistic analysis. Mc Dowell agrees with Kolodny who claims that black feminist criticism would be "short sighted if it summarily rejected all the inherited tools of critical analysis simply because they are male and western" (Eagleton 232). Black feminist critics should expose the oppression of sex, race and economy that gravely affected the experience and culture of black women. Barbara Christian observes in "But What Do We Think We Are Doing Anyway", "For me, doing black feminist criticism involved a literary activism that went beyond the halls of academe, not because I had so legislated but because in practice that is what it offers happily, had to be" (47).

In "Race for Theory", Barbara Christian contends that the black folk are a race for theory. They have always theorized. But their way of the theorizing is quite different from the western way. Their theorizing is in the form of narrative, in stories, riddles, and proverbs and in a special use of language. Black women use pithy language to unmask the assault on them. Their language is sensual, abstract, beautiful and communicative. The reigning academic intellectuals could not appreciate black literature. Black feminists struggled to make their voices heard. Literary critics have succeeded in silencing black creative writers. The language used in literary circles, says Christian, puzzles black writers.

Established critics often ask the black folk to produce a black feminist literary theory. Such a theory should be related to practice. Black women's literature is a collective endeavor and in their works we find an intersection of language, class, race and gender.

For Christian, "literature is a way of knowing that I am not hallucinating, that whatever I feel know 'is'" (21). Black literature is the literature of the subjugated people and has always been in danger of extinction. Black women's literature, says Christian, indicates the ways by which they theorize. Black critics and creative writers should achieve power and at the same time try to overcome the power that controlled them. Many black feminist critics including Audre Lorde have spoken of the need for cooperation, and the empowerment of black women.

Female feminists often question the involvement of males in feminist criticism. Michael Awkward's study on Afro-American women novelists, *Inspiring Influence,* was severely criticized. A male feminist critic is influenced by his own life experiences in shaping his perceptions and beliefs. Both male and female critics have explored the place of man in feminist criticism. The sincere involvement of black males in the field of feminism is often met with suspicion. One of the projects of black feminism is to find out the tradition of black female authors. When black males seriously set out to discover a black female literary tradition, they are regarded as unfit for such a task.

The efforts of male critics were dismissed as 'male readings' of female texts. Male feminists are regarded as 'not so feminist' because they are biologically male. Awkward cites Stephen Heath who insist that men's relation to feminism is an impossible one, "any notion of writing a feminist book or being a feminist, is a myth, a male imaginary with the reality of appropriation and domination right behind" (James and Sharply-Whiting 93).

Womanhood allows one to become a feminist but such a status is denied to men. Men cannot control nor overthrow the ideology of feminism. The ideology of feminism is able to withstand men's powerful acts of subversion. Black feminist literary critics take into account the role of black men in the subjugation of black women. Therefore black feminists do not regard the contribution made by black males as significant. In "Gender and Afro-Americanist Literary Theory and Criticism", Valery Smith suggests that black male critics and theorists "might explore the nature of the contradictions that arise when they undertake black feminist projects" (James and Sharpley-Whiting 95).

Alice Jardine opposes the involvement of men in feminism in "Men in Feminism: Odor di Uomo Or Campagnons de Route?" There is a struggle against patriarchy in feminist texts, which is absent in works by male feminists. Awkward quotes Jardine in his essay, "Why ... would men want to be in feminism if it's about struggle? What do men want to be in - in pain?" (James and Sharpley-Whiting 90). Addressing white male feminists Jardine asserts: "We do not want you to 'mimic' us, to become the same as us; we don't want your pathos or your guilt, and we don't even want your admiration (even if it is nice to get it once in a while). What we want, I would even say what we need, is your 'work'. We need you to get down to serious work. And like all serious work, that involves struggle and pain" (James and Sharpley-Whiting 95).

Many Afro-American males are hostile to contemporary black feminist literature. The works of black women are complex and diverse. When male critics analyse these works they concentrate on the presentation of black men. The subject of the writings of black women is their own life. But the male leaders and critics see it from a different perspective. As Deborah Mc Dowell says, "though black women writers have made black women the subjects of their own family stories, these male readers/critics are attempting to usurp that place for themselves and place it at the centre of critical inquiry" (84).

The representation of black men cannot be seen as an insignificant aspect of Afro-American women's texts. Black female critics and writers concentrate on black female subjectivity and experience. Black males instead of mimicking them should explore other areas of feminism. They should concentrate on topics such as obstacles to black male feminist endeavor, black male sexuality and so on. Black males and females should jointly participate in black feminist criticism.

Throughout generations women have been the victims of male physical and psychological cruelty. Awkward cites his mother's experience, "my father – who left us before I was one year old and whom I never knew - kicked her in the stomach when my fetal presence swelled her body, because he believed she'd been unfaithful to him and that I was only 'may be' his baby" (James and Sharpley-Whiting 100). Male feminists should participate in the endeavor of female feminists to dismantle phallocentrism. Afro-American male intellectuals have always tried to marginalize works by black women and black male critics should avoid this.

Bertha Harris explained lesbian literature at a Modern Language Association Convention in 1976. According to Harris, the sentence refuses to do what it is supposed to do in lesbian literature and there are strong images of women who refuse to be linear. Smith says that many of the works by black women writers are lesbian in this sense. Women are central figures and are positively portrayed and their relationship to each other is significant.

Barbara Smith examines the relationship between Sula and Nell in Toni Morrison's *Sula* and regards the novel as a lesbian one. Smith says that the near non-existence of black lesbian literature is due to the total suppression of all black women. In a speech on "The Autonomy of Black Lesbian Women", Wilmette Brown comments:

The isolation of black lesbian women, given that we are super freaks, given that our lesbianism defies both the sexual identity that capital gives us and the racial identity that capital gives us, the isolation of black lesbian women from heterosexual black women is very profound, very profound. I have searched throughout black history, black literature, whatever, looking for some women that I could see were somehow lesbian. Now I know that in a certain sense they were all lesbian. (19)

Gloria T. Hull at the University of Delaware discovered in the course of her research on black women poets of the Harlem Renaissance that many of the minor women writers of the period were in constant contact with each other. They provided both intellectual stimulation and psychological support for each other. Angelina Weld Grimké, a black woman writer, wrote many unpublished love poems to women.

Certain other critics opine that if the lesbian aspect of a work is given prominence, certain other aspects like its density and complexity, skillful blend of folklore, omens and symbolic richness will be ignored. Mc Dowell in her "New Directions for Feminist Criticism" quotes Annette Kolodny who warns feminist critics to be wary of "reading literature as though it was polemic". She says that "when using literary materials to make what is materially a political point" feminists find themselves "virtually rewriting a text, ignoring certain aspects of plot and characterization, or over-simplifying the action to fit our 'political' thesis". In such instances they "are neither practicing an honest criticism nor saying anything useful about the nature of art (or about the art of political persuasion, for that matter)" (28).

Politics is not an exclusively male domain in African societies. In some societies women occupy the highest political positions while in others their roles are limited. In some cases the public roles of women are concealed. Sometimes women who took on political roles were regarded as men. For instance, Sircar refers to Lovedu queens, the women monarchs who were sent 'wives' (31) by foreign and local thieves. The Queen kept a harem of men for her wives and the daughters of the wives could lay claims of heir ship to her throne.

In East Africa religion and politics were interdependent. Women enjoyed a position of equality with male monarchs when they became spirit mediums. Such women attained the position of chief and could judge trials. Colonialism brought a loss of political and economic status of African women. European colonizers failed to recognize the political role of African women. In Ghana and Nigeria women shared political power with men. In the colonial period men assumed all power. Women reacted against their loss of status. Women's war in 1929 was a response to the abrogation of rites. Referring to Judith Van Allen's "Aba Riots or Igbo Women's war? Ideology, Stratification and the Invisibility of Women", Roopali Sircar notes:

> Provoked by a move to tax their property, Igbo women, organised through their women's association (Mikiri) attacked the Warrant Chief whom they suspected of carrying out the taxation scheme and amassed in protest at the office. The British administration used police and soldiers and left more than 50 dead and 50 wounded. The 'disturbed area' covered 6000 square miles and the estimated number of women was in tens of thousands. The British used the term 'riots' and established the invisibility of these Igbo women. One would look in vain in the history books of Nigeria today for any mention that women were even involved. (31-32)

In traditional Igbo society, 'Omu' referred to the Igbo woman monarch while 'Obi' referred to the male monarch (32). Similarly, among the Ga of Ghana the father of the town 'mantse' shared power with 'manyei' (mother). Priests, elders, male and female captains all shared political power.

African women struggled against colonialism. Women took part in liberation movements. These liberation movements helped to alter the status of women. In regions like the Mozambique, Guinea Bissau and Zimbabwe, the liberation of women was regarded as a necessary step in social revolution. The liberation movements helped to transform social relations. Women assumed a variety of roles including that of warriors and wage earning members.

Along with men, African women also took part in struggles like Anza wan Freedom Movement, Mau Mau revolt, the Biafran wars, the Namibian Liberation Movement and in anti-apartheid demonstration in South Africa. Outstanding women activists include Winnie Mandela, Nomvo Bovi, Lilian Mesediba Ngogi and Sibongile Michabela. The Mozambique Liberation front (Frelimo) came into existence in exile in 1962. Women's liberation was one of its central issues. Women received political and military training and women took part in guerrilla warfare. They assumed roles closely allied to traditional male roles. Frelimo wanted women to participate in politics. Such transformation helped women to participate in all areas of work, to eradicate oppressive marriages and to provide increased educational opportunities to women.

The status of women deteriorated in newly independent African countries. The decline in women's status was due to male domination in the commercial sector and the importation of manufactured goods. Persons who held power were not interested in improving the status of women. The decline in women's status is seen even in most progressive African countries. The male dominated society reminded women that the object of a woman's life is to be a mother. Women were not allowed to make any progress in life. They suffered verbal and physical abuse and became victims of male expectations. In postcolonial Africa women underwent a second colonization. Their rights were not restored and government bureaucrats were insensitive to women's needs. African women were expected to uphold traditional values and to keep out of politics and issues like humans rights. Citing Christine Obbo, Sircar says:

> The unattached woman in urban Africa has come to be associated with premarital sex, pregnancy, illegitimacy, prostitution and violent crimes. A progressive and intelligent woman in East Africa who participates in politics would be regarded as a hooligan. Even in university circles men yawn and smirk when a woman discusses a political issue, and remind her that she talks too much. (38)

In a male dominated society women assume a silent stance. This is due to the political dominance of man and the lack of confidence of women.

Black women have a different view of themselves and their knowledge is independent of the established social order. Black feminist theory is based on the elements and themes of black women's culture. Black feminist views are based on the experiences of black women. The reality experienced by the dominated is different from that experienced by the subordinate. The techniques adopted by white feminists are different from that adopted by black feminists.

Within the white male controlled society the general notions are that of black and female inferiority. The black feminist theories that violated these fundamental assumptions put forward by white males were regarded as anomalies. White males were not familiar with the reality experienced by black women. Black women were denied educational positions and influential administrative positions. Black women's knowledge was not regarded as valuable.

The few black women who attain positions of authority are forced to use their authority to exclude the views of the majority of black women. As Patricia Hill Collins observes in "Social Construction of Black Feminist Thought":

One way of excluding the majority of black women from the knowledge-validation process is to permit a few black women to acquire positions of authority in institutions that legitimate knowledge and to encourage them to work within the taken-for-granted assumptions of black female inferiority shared by the scholarly community and the culture at large. Those black women who accept these assumptions are likely to be rewarded by their institutions, often at significant personal cost. Those challenging the assumptions run the risk of being ostracized. (James and Sharpley-Whiting 188)

Though black women share some of the experiences of white Western feminists most of the difficulties are unique. Black women are more oppressed than any other subjugated group. In the process of creating theory they cannot distance themselves from their experiences.

Subjugated groups often undergo similar types of oppression. Colonialism, imperialism, slavery and apartheid were the common modes of oppression suffered by black men and women. Feminists claim that all women irrespective of race, class and religion share a common patriarchal oppression. Though there are similarities in the oppression of black women, black men and white women, the experience of black women who are more oppressed than any other group is unique.

Women's writing reflects their experience. Transferring one's own experiences into literature does not require great academic knowledge. Collins refers to Ruth Shays who uses her concrete experiences to challenge the idea that formal education is the only route to knowledge:

I am the kind of person who doesn't have a lot of education, but both my father and my mother had good common sense. Now I think that is all you need. I might not know how to use thirty-four words where three would do, but that does not mean that I don't know what I'm talking about ... I know what I'm talking about because I'm talking about myself. I am talking about what I have lived. (James and Sharpley-Whiting 193)

Collins also refers to the subtitle of a work by Elsa Barkley Brown, "How my mother taught me to be a historian in spite of my academic training". Collins claims that African women are related to each other. Black women's tradition of sisterhood is based on their common experience.

The origin of contemporary black feminism is in the continuous struggle for survival and liberation of black women. Contemporary black feminism arose from the militancy and struggle of thousands of known and unknown black women activists. Racism and other forces have obscured the participation of black women in the feminist movement. Black feminists were active participants in movements like civil rights, Black Nationalism and Black Panthers. These activists felt the need to develop an anti-racist and anti-sexist politics.

2

Representation of Women in Buchi Emecheta's Second-Class Citizen and The Joys of Motherhood

Florence Onyebuchi ('Buchi') Emecheta was born in Lagos, Nigeria in 1944. Her childhood was divided between Lagos and Ibuza. She attended the Methodist Girl's High School in Lagos. Her parents Alice Ogbanje Ojebeta and Jeremy Nwabudike died when she was very young. She was educated on scholarship in Methodist Girls' High School. In school she was made to ask God's forgiveness for wanting to be a writer. Emecheta has written more than a dozen novels.

After marrying Sylvester Onwordi in 1960 she worked briefly at the US Embassy there. Sylvester migrated to London to pursue his studies. Two years later Emecheta joined her husband in London with her two children. She received a bachelor's degree in Sociology from the University of London. She had five children at the age of 22. Her husband burned the manuscript of her first novel *The Bride Price* and the incident was followed by their separation. The novel was rewritten and published in 1976. She states in her autobiography, *Head above Water* that she felt like the native, bush, independent woman. She packed her dripping four siblings and pregnant self and faced the streets of London.

She struggled hard, worked at odd jobs and wrote in the morning before work. She gained recognition with her article in the *New Statesman*, "Observations of the London poor". It became her first novel *In the Ditch* (1972), which dealt with her own story of lonely struggle with poverty in London and the difficulties of adjusting to a different culture. *Second-class citizen* (1974) is an autobiographical account of her marriage break-up. It reveals her determination to write and the struggles she had to face in an alien country. *The Slave Girl* (1977) won the Jock Campbell Award for Britain's most promising writers. The novel was based partly on the life experiences of Emecheta's mother, Alice Ogbanje Ojebeta Emecheta. The novel, *The Joys of Motherhood* portrays her Nigerian mother-in-law with warmth and compassion. It deals with the sufferings experienced by women who try to fulfill the role of 'complete' women by becoming perfect mothers and wives.

Emecheta gives a firsthand account of war in *Destination Biafra*. In Ibuza many of her friends and relatives died on account of war. Her niece-namesake perished of starvation. She was greatly influenced by her Nigerian compatriot, Flora Nwapa. Emecheta refers to herself as Nwapa's 'new sister'. Emecheta's novels include *In the Ditch, Second-class Citizen, The Bride Price, The Slave Girl, The Joys of Motherhood, Destination Biafra, Naira Power, Double Yoke, Gwendolen, The Rape of Shavi* and

Kehinde. Emecheta also wrote books for children. *Titch the Cat* (1980) was inspired by her daughter Alice's diary, *Nowhere to Play*, and by her daughter Christy's story of their life in a London County Council housing project. Her most widely acclaimed novel is *The Joys of Motherhood.*

Double Yoke (1982) is based on Emecheta's lectures and her stay at Calaba University. *The Rape of Shavi* (1983) is a science fiction satire. She has written plays for the BBC and scripted a book of photographs on Third World Women, *Our Own Freedom*, 1981. In her best works, she deals with the victimization of Nigerian women at home and abroad. She published her autobiography, *Head above Water* in 1994. *Head above Water* and *Kehinde* are set in London. Kehinde deals with gender relations.

Emecheta's works are based on her experiences as a young student and working mother as well as on the experiences of other African women. The sufferings of African women are dealt with compassion and realism. She took her M.Phil in social education and completed her Ph.D. in 1991. According to Emecheta she "integrates the profession of a writer into the cultural concept of mother / worker" (par. 20).

As Florence Stratton has stated in *Contemporary African Literature and the Politics of Gender,*

> Critics generally view Emecheta's novels as providing an authentic representation of African women ... (through) her portrayal of ... social and historical context. In *The Joys of Motherhood* this contextualization ... constitutes Emecheta's strongest statement in response to male idealizations of motherhood. (113)

Her works dealt with the themes of child slavery, motherhood, female independence and freedom through education. In her fiction she dealt with the problems of sexual discrimination and racial prejudice based on her experiences both as a single parent and black woman living in U.K.

Encyclopedia Britannica describes her writings as "stories of the world … [where] …women face the universal problems of poverty and oppression, and the longer they stay, no matter where they have come from originally, the more the problems become identical". In "Beyond Imperial Feminism: Buchi Emecheta's London Novels and the Black British Women's Emancipation", Ashley Dawson refers to her as "the first successful black woman novelist living in Britain after 1948" (117).

From 1965 to 1969, Emecheta worked as a library officer for the British Museum in London. From 1969 to 1976 she was a youth worker and sociologist for the Inner London Education Authority. Later she worked as a community worker in Camden, North London. Following her success as an author she travelled widely as a visiting professor and lecturer. She lectured at Yale University and University of London and became a Fellow at the University of London in 1986. She received the Jock Campbell Award from the *New Statesman* in 1978 for her novel *The Slave Girl* and was on Granta magazine's 1983 list of 20 "Best of Young British Novelists". She worked with many cultural and literary organizations including the Africa Centre, London. She received an honorary doctorate of literature from Farleigh Dickinson University in 1992. Emecheta features at number 98 on a list of 100 women recognized in August 2018 by BBC History Magazine as having changed the world. She suffered a stroke in 2010 and she died in London on 25 January 2017, aged 72. In 2017, Emecheta's son, Sylvester Onwordi announced the formation of The Buchi Emecheta Foundation, a charitable organization for promoting literary and educational projects in the UK and in Africa.

Julie Holmes in an interview with Emecheta asked her about the issue of feminism in her novels. She claims, "I work towards the liberation of women, but I'm not feminist. I'm just a woman" (par 24). She was able to transform her dreams into reality. She states, "Just keep trying and trying. If you have the determination and commitment, you will succeed" (par.25). She is an Ibo woman, an immigrant, a mother, and a writer. Her novels are autobiographical, historical, political and romantic. Like Toni Morrison she also believes that "fiction has a vital social responsibility" (par 6). Igbo qualities of vividness, economy and directness are found in her work. Her novels entertain and instruct with materials drawn directly from her life. She speaks for the marginalized black women and focuses upon the lives of black immigrant women. When Emecheta was asked about the use of the autobiographical form in her fictional works, she states, "Well, I admit that I am not very creative. I have to experience something or know someone who has seen something in order to write convincingly. People keep on going back to them (the autobiographical books) because when they read them they see a mirror of their own lives" (par 18).

She uses autobiography to give a true picture of the world in which she lives. She performed her roles as a mother, student, worker and writer equally well. In the interview she states, "If I was not to perish here, I realized that I had to find something I was good at. My books are about survival, just like my own life" (par18). When she was asked how she managed to write with the children she quietly replied that she had to write because of them. She recounted her experience of visiting a psychiatric hospital in London. "Out of the eleven patients, nine were black" (par 12). These people did not actually suffer from any mental sickness. They said that they heard voices and spoke to that voice. They spoke of their 'chi'(or spirit) and this in materialistic Britain, was regarded as a sign of insanity.

In her literary works Emecheta combines the cultural aspects of both Britain and Africa. She claims that "In all my novels I deal with the many problems and prejudices which exists for black people in Britain today" (par 7). She is deeply interested in her culture and her writing. Through her novels she highlights the problems of black people and makes their voices heard. She claims, "I believe it is important to speak to your readers in person ... to enable people to have a whole picture of me; I have to both write and speak. I view my role as a writer and also as oral communicator" (par 10). She is very much attached to her native land, Nigeria. Julie Holmes says that Emecheta returns to Nigeria for three to six months each year. In Emecheta's own words, "I keep my two worlds, my two cultures" (par 15). Much of Emecheta's fiction is set in Ibuza early in the twentieth century. She views her writing as "the release for all my anger, all my bitterness, my disappointments, my questions and my joy" (par 5).

She has written numerous plays as well as children's books for the BBC. She has set up her own publishing firm, Ogwugwu Afor, named after a strong Ibo goddess. She provided help and financial support to black artists. She claims that her early life in London was both financially and emotionally a hard one. She went to England to fulfill her father's wish that a member of his family should visit the 'kingdom of God' (England). *Second-class Citizen* deals with her experiences in England. The novel is autobiographical and portrays the circumstances that led to the breakup of her marriage.

Black women mostly deal with their own lives in their works. Though black men and black women are oppressed, women are hit particularly hard. At least some African women refuse to accept a status secondary to black men. They resisted their subjugation with their inner strength. Through the story of Adah, Emecheta tries to make the readers familiar with the realities of black women's lives. *Second-class Citizen* tells the story of Adah, a woman from the Ibo tribe, from her childhood till the breakup in her marriage.

Adah is not certain about her age. Nobody thought of recording her birth because she was 'only a girl'. She was born when her parents were expecting a boy. She was as insignificant as any other African girl. A girl child is marginalized and is 'available' to males. Adah's younger brother, Boy was sent to Ladi-Lak Institute, an expensive school. Adah could not attend the school because she was a girl. So she secretly went to the Methodist school where her neighbor Mr.Cole taught. Her mother was charged with child neglect and taken to the police station and forced to drink uncooked 'gaari' there. Adah was very good at her studies. She passed the entrance examination to the school of her dreams and even won a scholarship meant for the best five children. She was able to get jobs in London because of her education.

Women see themselves as insignificant. They have little choice but to accept the roles assigned to them by society. Adah felt uncomfortable even with her mother. "She thought that it was these experiences with Ma so early in life that had given her such a very low opinion of her own sex. ... Women still made Adah nervous. They had a way of sapping her self confidence" (6). Society regarded the girl as a second-class human being. She is not even a complete human being. Even though Adah was educated she could not liberate her mind from the constraints imposed by society and she felt that she was powerless to shatter its false values.

When her son, Vicky was admitted to the Royal free Hospital, a nurse asked Adah whether Vicky was her only child. Adah replied that she had another. But that was 'only a girl'. The nurse tried to make her understand that she should not differentiate between her children. To quote from the novel,

> Adah knew all that. But how was she to tell this beautiful creature that in her society she could only be sure of the love of her husband and the loyalty of her parents-in-law by having and keeping alive as many children as possible, and that though

a girl may be counted as one child, to her people a boy was like four children put together? And if the family could give the boy a good university education, his mother would be given the status of a man in the tribe. How was she to explain all that? That her happiness depended so much on her son staying alive. (62)

Even though Adah paid for the plans, decisions in the household were often made behind her back. Women did not get to know about important decisions in the household until after these were discussed among the men folk. Emecheta reveals the arrogance and folly of men whose selfish desires are sanctioned by religion and culture. The silent suffering, the anger, hurt, pain and frustration of Adah is also exposed. Adah suffered not from any fault of her own, but simply because she is a black woman. She was a double nonentity. She was rejected by the white British society as well as by her black husband. As a black woman, Adah was oppressed by white women, white men and black men.

Black women were always victims. Adah never got any peace and comfort in her married life. Her husband, Francis needed victims and Adah was his victim but not a willing one. The only comfort in her life was her children. She refused to be the silent suffering wife and remained a fighter till the end. She took on the sole responsibility of her children, used her sound intelligence and emerged triumphant.

Mother-child relationship is a central theme in African literature. Marriage fulfills a woman's biological need for procreation. It also emphasizes the inferior status of woman. Polygamy provides the male with the power to marry a number of women. Throughout generations, women have been the victims of physical and psychological cruelty. Maleness was usually expressed in violence and brutality. Most black women who were powerless against phallocentric rule accepted the social roles without protest.

Though Adah was married to Francis, he never treated her as his equal. She was denied the rights and privileges of a wife. Instead, it was her money that bound her to him. She was harassed mentally, physically and emotionally. Linda Martin Alcoff in "Racism" cites Ann Ferguson who refers to the different forms of patriarchy. One form of patriarchy is the 'father right' where the father controlled the resources available to the child. In 'husband right', the husbands who earned money subjugated their wives. Ferguson refers to public patriarchy where the state administers resources on the basis of rules that control women. In the novel, Francis, the unemployed husband, tortures his wage earning wife. He is tied to her because of her salary. He tortures her physically and mentally because he is confident that she will not leave him, as he is the father of her children.

Francis quoted the Bible to remind his wife that she was inferior to him. He told her that she was called 'wo-man' because she was made from the rib of a man. Adah listened silently though she knew that Francis' story couldn't be applicable to the Igbo words 'opoho' which meant woman and 'okei' which meant man. It was man who was always 'rational' and 'intelligent' and so Francis reminded Adah about the need to be a 'virtuous' woman whose price was above rubies.

In Francis' view, a wife was the slave of the husband. Their marriage day is referred to as 'the saddest day in Adah's whole life' (20). She realized that she had made a mistake in marrying him. She married him because she needed a home. Her dream of migrating to the United Kingdom would not have become a reality without her marriage because it was difficult for single girls to go to England. Adah was an expensive bride because she was college educated. Her mother searched for the highest bidder. Though she tried to love and respect Francis, she could not do that because he had none of the qualities that commanded love and respect:

To him, a woman was a second class human, to be slept with at any time, even during the day, and, if she refused, to have sense beaten into her until she gave in, to be ordered out of bed after he had done with her, to make sure she washed his clothes and got his meals ready at the right time. There was no need to have an intelligent conversation with his wife because, you see, she might start getting ideas. Adah knew she was a thorn in his flesh. (175)

She recognized him as her enemy who could kill her any moment and make the world believe that it was an accident:

She gave in to his demands for the sake of peace. They were like the "demands of a wicked child who enjoys torturing a live animal given to him as a pet" (162). When she could not endure anymore beatings, she started hitting him back. She could not regard Francis as her master and herself as his slave. In the library whenever girls talked about love and marriage, Adah never opened her mouth because she did not want to spoil their dreams by revealing the reality that "marriage was not a bed of roses but tunnel of thorns, fire and hot nails". (42)

Francis told Adah that he had married her because she could work harder than other girls and because she was orphaned very early in life. For him, marriage meant lots of sex and nothing more. He liked variety and believed that men had the right to possess as many women as they pleased. Their custom allowed it. He searched for and even chased other women. Adah encouraged this in order to get herself some peace.

Men can never do wrong. This is an unwritten rule voiced by Okpara. When Okpara, a black Igbo man finds Adah crying silently, he guesses that she had quarreled with her husband. He tells her:

I don't want to hear anything. Let's go and beg his forgiveness. He would let you in. It's typical Igbo psychology; men never do wrong, only the women; they have to beg for forgiveness, because they are bought, paid for and must remain like that, silent obedient slaves. (164)

Okpara advised Francis to work for his family so that he could gain the respect of his sons. He did not mention Titi, the daughter because she was only a girl, a second class human being and not a complete human like a man. Boys were regarded as special, super human beings and they grew up to become self-centered men like Francis. Emecheta has not portrayed all black men as equally bad. Her characters are convincingly portrayed as she drew her materials directly from life. Adah's own father, Pa, can be sharply contrasted with her husband Francis. Pa loved her very much and she knew that she had to suffer early in her life due to the death of her father.

Adah's victim status is related to motherhood. She is not, however, the passive, silent victim when her children are in danger. When Vicky falls ill she tells Francis:

If anything happens to my son, I am going to kill you and that prostitute. You sleep with her, do you not? You buy her pants with the money I work for, and you both spend the money I pay her, when I go to work. I don't care what you do, but I must have my children whole and perfect. The only thing I get from this slavish marriage is the children. And Francis I am warning you, they must be perfect children. (63-64)

Francis could never enslave Adah. He never succeeds in subjugating her completely. Though physically weaker, she is mentally and emotionally superior to Francis. Adah realized that she never got any love, safety or security out of marriage. She endured all her suffering because Francis was the father of her children. He too knew that she could not leave him because of the children. Francis tells Okpara, "She simply went out. I did not know where, but I knew she would come back because she can't bear to leave her children for long. I did not beat her. Did she say that?" (167).

At twenty one, Adah had three children. She tried birth control. Francis hit her and abused her in front of other tenants and Pa Noble. According to Francis, the cap that Adah tried was invented for harlots and single women. He enjoyed torturing Adah. She was like a live animal under his control. The severity of the violence that she endured is revealed when she says that,

> She was happy when Pa Noble came, because at least it made Francis stop hitting her. She was dizzy with pain and her head throbbed. Her mouth was bleeding. And once or twice during the proceedings she felt tempted to run out and call the police. But she thought better of it. Where would she go after that? She had no friends and she had one relation in London. (155)

Adah's ability to withstand and oppose repressive circumstances is evident from her novel, *The Bride Price.* With her strength and courage she survived the harshness of life. As the Deborah Mc Dowell says in "Reading Family Matters", "... if we can claim a center for these texts, it is located in the complexities of black female subjectivity and experience" (James and Sharpley-Whiting 96). Emecheta portrays in the novel her husband's destruction of her own first novel. Adah's work is appreciated by her friends who read it. Francis who was a failure never wanted Adah to rise above him. He was a failure in his role as son, husband, father and a student. He would do everything to make Adah to a failure like himself. He could not help it, it was human nature (167).

For Francis, Adah was only a black woman who could not write anything valuable. "Francis could never tolerate an intelligent woman" (178). Adah's 'brainchild' was nothing but 'rubbish' for him. He burned her story with great delight. For him Adah is merely a "brainless creature" (178). Alice Walker speaks of the psychic toll on black women who do not find an outlet for their talents. In the essay, "In Search of

Our Mother's Gardens" she states that black women are "driven to a numb and bleeding madness by the springs of creativity in them for which there is no release" (Eagleton 34). Adah dreamt of becoming a writer and after writing her first novel *The Bride Price* she found mental peace and relief amidst all her worries. Adah's novel was her brainchild. When Francis burnt her novel she realized that all her dreams and all her hopes were shattered. She then knew that Francis could kill her children and the incident led to their separation.

Inspired by Marx, Adah determines to leave Francis with her children because "she had nothing to lose but her chains" (161). After a fight, Adah moved to her new house with her four babies. Francis did not want to be separated from her. She was his slave. He goes to Adah's new house. To quote from the novel,

> What followed is too horrible to print. Adah remembered, though, that during the confusion Francis told her he had a knife. He now carried knives with him. She tried several times to call for help, but could feel the life being squeezed out of her. She then heard people talking, banging the door which Francis had locked. But the landlord had guessed that Francis was Adah's husband and, like most of his people, he didn't want to interfere until a real murder had been committed. (183)

Apart from the oppression of black men, black women suffered the oppression of white men and women. When Adah came to London, the land of her dreams, the reality filled her with horror. England gave Adah a cold welcome. Francis even lifted his hands to hit Adah. Francis was free from parental control and could do whatever he wished. Their home was itself a horror. Francis reminded Adam of their subordination, "you may be living like elite, but the day you land in England, you are a second-class citizen. So you can't discriminate against your own people, because we are all second-class" (36-37).

The white British society hated black people, particularly black women. Black women could do nothing to alter their political or cultural oppression. White signified purity while black denoted evil. White women, who were often oppressed because of their gender, acted as oppressors of black people. White women projected themselves as powerless, passive victims. They were, however, oppressors of black women although they did not acknowledge it. Racism played a crucial role in the oppression of blacks, particularly black women. White women had power over black men and they too had a role in promoting racism.

White is placed in direct opposition to black. White symbolizes purity and black represents evil. As Simone De beauvoir asserts in the poem "Dictionary Black":

A Darky is a negro
Not fair-atrocious-evil
And the prince of Darkness
Is the Devil...
... So I turn to 'white'
All sweetness and light. (Eagleton 333)

Adah's search for a house proved extremely difficult because almost all the advertisements said "Sorry, No Coloureds." She phoned a white landlady and spoke to her with her nostrils pressed together so that she may not sound African. The woman was very friendly one and invited Adah and her husband to come. When she saw their faces, however,

the woman clutched at her throat with one hand, her little mouth opening and closing as if gasping for air, and her bright kitten like eyes dilated to the fullest extent. She has made several attempts to talk but no sound came. Her mouth had obviously gone dry. (78)

She told them that the rooms had just been taken. She asked them to search elsewhere and Adah was shocked at this rejection.

This was contrary to Adah's views about whites. The black people of Ibuza, respected the whites. They warmly welcomed the lawyer Nweze who had returned from the United Kingdom. They believed that the whites could never do any wrong. When Adah came into contact with the whites, she realized that the blacks were completely mistaken in such notions. She realized that the concept of 'whiteness' could cover a multitude of sins (44).

In England, Africans were regarded as second-class citizens. Their children had to be fostered. Trudy was the foster mother of Adah's children. One day when Adah visited Trudy, she found Vicky pulling rubbish out of the bin and Titi washing her hands and face with the water leaking from the toilet. Adah reported the matter to the children's officer and Trudy went there in floods of tears. She convinced them that Adah's children had wandered into the backyard because she had a 'stinking' visitor who refused to go. Adah knew the 'visitor' was her husband. Trudy was a registered daily minder. Though Trudy was reprimanded, Adah then learnt that the notion that the whites never lied was a myth.

In "New Directions for Black Feminist Criticism", Deborah E. Mc Dowell refers to the motif of journey in the works of black women writers. She says that the journey of black men is a "descent into the underworld" (Bobo 233) which is found in Ralph Ellison's *Invisible Man*, Imamu Amiri Baraka's *The System of Dante's Hell* and Richard Wright's "The Man who Lived Underworld". The journey of the female is from "victimization to consciousness" (233). In the novel we witness to Adah's personal and psychological Journey. She moves from 'victimization to consciousness'. She suffered racial and sexual oppression while in London. When she came to London, she was made to believe that her color was something to be ashamed of. Later, when she became conscious of her victimization, she achieves self-realization. Her indomitable spirits refused to be subdued. She rose to every challenge. "She was different. Her children were going to be different. They were all going to be black, they were going to enjoy being black, be proud of being black, a black of a different breed. That's what they were going to be" (148).

The Joys of Motherhood is regarded as more technically refined than Emecheta's first novel. Katherine Fishburn in *Reading Buchi Emecheta: Cross-cultural Conversations* regarded it as her 'most controversial' novel. Some feminist critics even questioned Emecheta's commitment to feminism. This is because Nnu Ego, her heroine failed to escape her oppression. Laura Franey refers to the opinion of a male critic that the portrayal of men in the novel was exaggerated. The novel has incorporated Igbo story telling practices. Franey cites Susan Ardnt who, in "Buchi Emecheta and the Tradition of Ifo: Continuation and Writing Back", compares Emecheta's narrative techniques with those employed by female story tellers in Igbo villages.

The writings of Emecheta and Chinua Achebe show their concern for the survival and well-being of the Igbo people. Okonkwo in *Things Fall Apart* and Nnu Ego in *The Joys of Motherhood* combine the positive and negative aspects of the tribal culture. Their own struggles to survive anticipate Nigeria's struggle for political independence. *Things Fall Apart* takes place in the 1890s and *The Joys of Motherhood* in the middle of the twentieth century. Colonization and Christianity threaten Okonkwo's traditional beliefs. He is paralyzed by the changes. Nnu Ego is the daughter of the local chief Agbadi and she follows the traditions and customs to the bitter end. Her traditional beliefs and customs have little relevance in the colonial environment. Unlike Nnu Ego, Adaku, Nnaife's second wife adapts to modern needs. Her behavior as a good, traditional wife unwittingly lands Nnaife in prison. Her eldest son, Oshia rejects tradition outright. Oshia was responsible for his parents' wellbeing. But he rejects his aged parents. Although this pained Nnu Ego she could not blame Oshia. According to John Updike, there is a plain feminist message borne by Ona and enacted by Adaku that women must seize the right to control their lives when they can, if they and their people are to survive.

The master-slave relationship is the most prominent one in the novel. Slavery is evident in the relationship between whites and blacks, husband and wife and even in mother's love for the child. Nnaife is the owner of his wives. He owned Nnu Ego because he had paid her bride price. He tells her, "Did I not pay your bride price? Am I not your owner?" (48). A woman is regarded as a property, which can be transferred from one person to another. When a man dies his wives are to be inherited by the man's brother or other male relatives. Nnaife inherited the wives of his brother. Nnu Ego accepted her role as a slave both to her husband as well as to her children. At the time of her husband's trial she says, "Nnaife is the head of our family. He owns me, just like God in the sky owns us. So even though I pay the fees, yet he owns me. So in other words he pays" (217). She links the power of the husband over his wife to that of God over human beings.

Nnu Ego does not directly challenge slavery. But she prays to God for her personal freedom:

God, when will you create a woman who will be fulfilled in herself, a full human being, not anybody's appendage?" She prayed desperately "After all, I was born alone, and I shall die alone. What have I gained from all this? Yes, I have many children, but what do I have to feed them on? On my life I have to work myself to the bone to look after them, have to give them my all. And if I am lucky enough to die in peace, I even have to give them my soul. They will worship my dead spirit to provide for them: it will be hailed as a good spirit so long as there are plenty of yams and children in the family, but if anything should go wrong, if a young wife does not conceive or if there is a famine; my dead spirit will be blamed. When will I be free? (186 to 187)

Nnu Ego will never be free. She is bound by slavery in life as well as in death. She never voices her dissatisfaction unlike Adaku who openly rebels against her slavery. She turns into a prostitute in order to provide a good education to her girl children, to enjoy more freedom and to release herself from the bondage of slavery. She soon earned enough money and owned a large market stall. She could send both her girls to excellent schools. She reminds Nnu Ego that the older ways of society do not have the same force they once had: "Nnaife does not own anybody, not in Nigeria today. But, senior wife, don't worry. You believe in the tradition. You have changed a little, but stood firm by your belief" (218).

Nnu Ego's father, Nwokocha Agbadi, was a local chief. He owned many slaves. When Agbadi's senior wife died, her personal slave was supposed to accompany her to the grave. When she refused, Agbadi's eldest son gave her a blow on the head with his cutlass and killed her. Later Nnu Ego realizes that her husband and other black men were slaves to the white men:

Are we not all slaves to the white men, in a way? asked Nnu Ego in a strained voice. "If they permit us to eat, then we will eat. If they say we will not then where will we get the food? Ubani, you are a lucky man and I am glad for you. The money may be small, and the work slave labour, but at least your wife's mind is at rest knowing that at the end of the month she gets some money to feed her children and you. What more does a woman want? (117)

The Britishers forced Nnaife and his colleagues to join the army. The blacks knew that the British owned them just like God did. The British were free to take any of them wherever they wished. Dr. Meers for whom Nnaife worked laughed at him, calling him a baboon.

Emecheta depicts colonialism as ownership in the novel. Like women, men are also portrayed as slaves. Nnu Ego says that Nigerian men who do menial work for Englishmen are slaves. Colonialism meant the illegal ownership of one group of human beings by another. The story takes place in Nigeria under British rule, before independence.

Yet another form of slavery depicted is mother's love for her children. Nnu Ego knew that she was imprisoned by her love for her children. However, great her suffering was, a woman could never leave her children. "Her love and duty for her children were like her chain of slavery (186). Women were cleverly enslaved by men who understood this. Even when Oshia refuses to help his mother and his family, Nnu Ego tells her son Adim,

> And don't forget Osha is my son, just like you. Some fathers, especially those with many children from different wives, can reject a bad son, a master can reject his evil servant, a wife can even leave a bad husband, but a mother can never, never reject her son. If he is damned, she is damned with him ... (214).

As Filomena Chioma Steady in *The Black Women Cross Culturally* has noted,

> The most important factor with regard to the woman in traditional society is her role as mother and the centrality of this role as a whole. Even in strictly patrilineal societies women are important as wives and mothers since their reproduction capacity is crucial to the maintenance of the husband's lineage and it is because of women that men can have a patrilineage at

all. The importance of motherhood and the evaluation of the child bearing capacity by African women is probably the most fundamental difference between the African woman and her Western counterpart in their common struggle to end discrimination against women. (163)

In her autobiography, *Head above Water*, Emecheta states that she had created a woman, Nnu Ego, who gave up everything she had to raise her kids. Nnu Ego is a victim of her motherhood. Huma Ibrahim says in "Ontological Victimhood" that at the end of her life Nnu Ego becomes Helene Cixous's "sorceress ... and hysteric whose body is transformed into a theatre for forgotten scenes, relives the past, bearing witness to a lost childhood that survives in suffering" (155). As Emecheta says in *Head above Water*, Nnu Ego gave up everything for the sake of her children. But her motherhood is used to victimize her. If at first she suffered due to lack of progeny, she suffers later due to a relative abundance of progeny.

Nnu Ego's first husband, Amatokwu told her that he could not waste his 'precious seeds' (32) on a barren woman. When his second wife conceives, Nnu Ego is further humiliated. The bride price he had paid was returned to him and he was relieved to rid of her. Later she becomes a prolific producer of children after her marriage to Nnaife. Adaku, the junior wife who does not have any male children, is jealous of her. Adaku gives birth to a son but the child dies soon. Nnu Ego goes to Ibuza where she witnesses the death of her ailing father. When she returns to Lagos after eight months she finds herself poor while Adaku is a prosperous trader. Nnu Ego ill-treated a lady who had come to visit a Adaku. Adaku appealed for justice to the male relatives. They blamed Adaku because she had no son and had no right to complain about the conduct of the senior wife. Nnu Ego was declared innocent because she was the mother of sons. Even Nnu Ego felt sorry for Adaku.

When Nnu Ego lost her first son, Ngozi she attempts suicide. Patriarchal society dictates that women should aspire for children or die. When Nnu Ego lost her first son she had failed to live up to the expected standards of her society. The significance of motherhood for an African woman is highlighted by Nnu Ego's statement, "But I am not a woman anymore. I am not a mother anymore. The child is there, dead on the mat" (62). The people who witness Nnu Ego's mental anguish agree that a woman without a child was a failure.

Even in her poverty Nnu Ego boasted of her sons. She told her friends what her sons were going to be when they grew up. People who did not have sons, or those who had only daughters, or those who had no children at all kept quiet. Nnu Ego points out to Adaku's daughter, Dumbi, that she must respect Oshia, because he was the heir and future owner of the family. When Nnu Ego gave birth to twin girls, Nnaife became happy because their bride prices could be used to pay the school fees of the boys. Even Adaku tells Oshia that he was "worth more than ten Dumbis" (128). Oshia is made to believe that he is special. Nnu Ego had great hopes and expectations about her eldest son Oshia. She, however, becomes pessimistic when Oshia refuses to help the younger children.

The patriarchal powers made Nnu Ego aware that her children were of great worth. The title *The Joys of Motherhood* is ironic because the only joy Nnu Ego derived from her motherhood is a fabulous funeral. She gave up everything she had for the sake of her children. In return she is rejected by her husband and betrayed by her children. Her death is described in an ironic vein:

> After such wandering on one night, Nnu Ego laid down by
> the roadside, thinking that she had arrived home. She died qui-
> etly there, with no child to hold her hand and no friend to talk

to her. She had never made many friends, so busy had she been building up her joys as mother. (224)

Even after her death she is regarded as a 'wicked woman' because "however many people appealed to her to make women fertile, she never did" (224). She perhaps becomes a rebel after her death because of her experience of the 'joys' of motherhood. As Huma Ibrahim states in "Ontological Victimhood",

> In Emecheta's *The Joys of Motherhood* and *In the Ditch*, childlessness as well as abundance of progeny seems to be the root cause of the suffering women victim ... In *The Joys of Motherhood*, Nnu Ego is victimized first by her inability to become a mother and later, because she is a mother. Lack or abundance of children suggests several ways in which the dominant power structure first tantalizes and then victimizes women. (156)

In her autobiography, *Head above Water,* Emecheta describes her clash with her eldest daughter, Chiedu, which had led to her writing of the novel. Chiedu had asked her mother to shift her to an expensive School. She refused to do so because of financial problems. Laura Franey notes in *World Literature and its Times* Vol.2, that in December 1976, Chiedu went to live with her father for some time. Emecheta "banged away (on the typewriter) the whole of Christmas, the whole of January 1977, by the end of that month, almost six weeks after Chiedu left, *The Joys of Motherhood* was finished" (233).

The Joys of Motherhood is different from African fiction by male writers. Male novelists depicted women either as the saintly mother or the debased prostitute. Laura Franey notes in *African Literature and its Times* that "*The Joys of Motherhood* provides a strong connective to novels authored by males because it realistically portrays the suffering experiences by women who try to fulfill the role of perfect mother and wife (233). Franey also compares Flora Nwapa's *Efuru* with Buchi Emecheta's *The Joys of Motherhood*. Emecheta's novel focuses on the lives of ordinary women. It deals with the positive and negative aspects of women's experiences. The protagonist in *Efuru* is relatively unconventional. *The Joys of Motherhood* portrays the suffering of a woman who tried to play the traditional role of a perfect mother and wife. Franey cites Florence Stratton's observation in *Contemporary African Literature and the Politics of Gender:*

> Critics generally view Emecheta's novels as providing an authentic representation of African women through her portrayal of the social and historical context. In *The Joys of Motherhood*, this contextualization ... constitutes Emecheta's strongest statement in response to male idealization of motherhood. (233)

Motherhood is the root cause of Nnu Ego's suffering: "if you don't have children the longing for them will kill you, and if you do, the worrying over them will kill you" (212). Nnu Ego's children meant everything to her. Taking the children away from her was like taking her life away.

Just as in motherhood, attitudes love, care, cooperation and support can be seen in the relations of women with each other. Like the critic Barbara Christian, one might also detect lesbian elements in *The Joys of Motherhood*. Barbara Smith in "Toward a Black Feminist Criticism" cites Bertha Harris's claim that in lesbian literature there are strong images of women who refuse to be linear. In lesbian literary works homosexuality is not of overwhelming importance. Here women are the central figures and their relationships are significant.

Emecheta portrays the co-operation and friendship among the African women in her novels. Even though there were minor jealousies and petty quarrels, these are soon forgotten and the women are united by the oppression they suffer. They provide both intellectual stimulation and psychological support to each other.

Adaku and Nnu Ego, for all their quarrels and jealousy, remain united in their suffering. They suffer from poverty as well as from the physical torture at the hands of Nnaife. They organize a 'cooking strike' to remind Nnaife of the consequences of his unwise spending. There are also other instances of women supporting each other in the novel. When Nnu Ego thanks Cordelia who had helped in her child birth, she says, "We are like sisters on a pilgrimage. Why should we not help one another?" (53). When Nnu Ego and her son Oshia fall in from malnutrition, a kind woman of the neighborhood, Iyawo Itsekiri, prepare delicious food for them. She did not want to make them feel that she was providing for them when they lacked food. Black women always supported each other because they had no other support. They were powerless before all men and white woman. When Nnu Ego was thrown out of Amatokwu's house hold because of her failure to produce a child, Agbadi's wives nursed her back to health: "Most of his wives, now elderly, were sympathetic and nursed her mentally back to normal. They made her feel that even though she had not borne a child, her father's house was bursting with babies she could regard as her own" (35).

Though mothers bestowed special care on their sons, they still loved their daughters. According to the rules of patriarchal society male children were special creatures. Adaku turns prostitute to provide a good education for her daughters. Nnu Ego too wished to give her girl children a good education although she lacked money. Nnu Ego asks, "But who made the law that we should not hope in our daughters?" (187).

Emecheta also examines the issues of poverty and unemployment that contribute to the suffering of black women. Nnu Ego's husband, Nnaife was the washerman of the English Meers couple. Nnu Ego did not approve of this work. When the white couple left for England,

Nnaife lost his job and remained unemployed for a while. They lived on Nnu Ego's meager income from the sale of cigarettes. When Nnaife's friend Ubani got a job Nnu Ego says, "Ubani you are a lucky man and I am glad for you. The money maybe small, and the work slave labor, but at least your wife's mind is at rest knowing that at the end of the month she gets some money to feed her children and you. What more does a woman want?" (117). Nnaife get a job as a grass cutter. He is forced into the army to fight for the British in World War II. Emecheta's father had fought in Burma just as Nnaife does in the novel. During Nnaife's absence, Nnu Ego went to Ibuza. When she returned to Lagos after her father's funeral she finds that her own poverty contrasts sharply with Adaku's prosperity from trade. She gathered, cut and sold firewood to pay the rent, feed the children and send the boys to school before she got the large sum of sixty pounds given to her as Nnaife's salary.

Nnu Ego's death is a brutal reminder of women's folly in devoting their whole life to their husbands and children. Emecheta portrays the pain and humiliation of women in a polygamous society. Nnu Ego's father, Nwokocha Agbadi had seven wives and a mistress apart from Nnu Ego's mother, Ona. When Nnu Ego failed to conceive, her first husband takes a younger wife. Her second husband, Nnaife Omulum, inherits several wives following the death of his brother.

Emecheta in her writings scan every aspect of the socio-political scene and its impact on women. Her writings gave rise to a new self-awareness among African women. As Chinua Achebe observes in "The African Writer and the Biafran Cause",

It is clear to me that an African creative writer who tries to avoid the big social and political issues of contemporary Africa will end up being completely irrelevant like that absurd man in the proverb who leaves his home burning to pursue a rat fleeing from the flames. (122)

Emecheta's story of African family life is closely connected with colonization and its impact. She exposes the power and authority of the white men over the lives of poor black people and also raises pertinent questions about traditional attitudes to womanhood.

3

Locating the Self in Flora Nwapa's Efuru

Florence Nwanzuruahu Nkiri Nwapa (13 January 1931- 16 October 1993) was a Nigerian author and is regarded as the mother of modern African literature. She was born in Oguta, in South eastern Nigeria and was the eldest of the six children of Christopher Ijeoma and Martha Nwapa. Her father was an agent with the United Africa Company and her mother was a teacher of drama. She earned a B.A. degree at the age of 26 from University College, Ibadan and then went to Scotland where she earned a diploma in education from Edinburgh University in 1958. She was married to Gogo Nwakuche and had three children Ejine, Uzoma and Amede. She achieved international recognition with her first novel, *Efuru* published in 1966 and was acknowledged as the first African woman novelist to be published in the English language in Britain. Her other novels are *Idu* (1970), *Never Again* (1975), *One is Enough* (1981) and *Women are Different* (1986). She published two col-

90

lections of stories: *This is Lagos* (1971) and *Wives at War* (1980) and the volume of poems, *Cassava Song and Rice Song* (1986). She also wrote several books for children: *The Adventures of Deke* (1980), *The Miracle Kittens* (1980), *Journey to Space* (1980), *Mammy water* (1979) and *Emeka, Driver's Guard* (1972). In an interview with *Contemporary Authors* she points out that she had been writing for nearly thirty years. She admits that her interest has been on both the rural and the urban woman in their quest for survival in a fast-changing world dominated by men.

Nwapa founded the Tana Press in the year 1974 and Flora Nwapa Company in 1977 for publishing her own adult and children's literature as well as works by other writers. She recreated life and traditions from an Igbo woman's viewpoint. In "Flora Nwapa and the Letter That Changed Nigerian Literature Forever" Tana has been described as the first press run by a woman and targeted at a large female audience. A project far beyond its time at a period when no one saw African women as constituting a community of readers or a book-buying demographic. In an interview in the Frankfurt Book Fair 1980 Nwapa pointed out as one her objectives to inform and educate women all over the world, especially Feminists (both with capital F and small f) about the role of women in Nigeria, their economic independence, their relationship with their husbands and children, their traditional beliefs and their status in the community as a whole.

She worked with the orphans and refugees who were displaced during the Biafran War. She worked as a school teacher at Queen's School in Enugu from 1959 to 1962. She held several positions including Assistant Registrar at the University of Lagos, Minister of Health and Social welfare in East Central State (1970-71), Minister of Lands, Survey and Urban Development (1971-74) and was a visiting lecturer at Alvan Ikoku College of education in Owerri, Nigeria. In 1989 she was appointed as a visiting professor of creative writing at University of Maiduguri. Nwapa died of pneumonia on 16 October 1993 at a hospital in Enugu, Nigeria at the age of 62.

Efuru, the protagonist was born into the highly respected Nwashike family. She is raised solely by her father, Nwashike Ogene a hero and leader of his tribe. He was praised for being wise and understanding. The story is set in West African Igbo rural community. The beautiful Efuru falls in love with a poor farmer, Adizua. She defies tradition and runs away with him although he cannot pay her dowry. She is presented as a beautiful, kind-hearted, strong-willed and free spirited woman. She helps her husband pay her bride price. Her mother-in-law, Ossai and Adizua's aunt, Ajanapu are very fond of her. But Adizua abandons Efuru and their daughter, Ogonim as his own father has done in the past. Later Ogonim dies and Efuru finds that Adizua has married another woman and had a child with her. He does not even return for their daughter's funeral. Adizua is portrayed as a lazy and irresponsible man unworthy to marry Efuru. Her mother-in-law did not want Efuru to leave and asks her to remain in waiting in their marital house. She waits for some time and later leaves his house and goes back to the house of her father. Her father appears very lenient when Efuru breaks tradition and receives her happily. Efuru then meets, Gilbert, an educated man of her age group. She marries him according the traditions. Initially their marriage appeared to be a happy one. But later her inability to conceive created troubles in their marriage. Efuru is chosen by the goddess of the lake, Uhamiri to be one of her worshippers. Uhamiri is known to offer wealth and beauty to her worshippers but few children. Efuru's second marriage too failed as Gilbert favoured his second and third wives.

The novel was a stepping stone in Nigerian literature and Nwapa was awarded the title "Ogbuefi", usually given to men. It meant "killer of cow". The Nigerian government granted her several prestigious awards after *Efuru* was released. The Kenyan author, Grace Ogot pointed out in a review of the novel that, "of the many novels that are coming out of Nigeria, *Efuru* is one of the few that portrays vividly the woman's world, giving only peripheral treatment to the affairs of men" (80). But several male critics like Eldred Jones criticized Nwapa for focusing on the affairs of women. Author Rose Acholonu describes Nwapa and certain African female writers as "pathfinders" who were able to "break the seals of silence and invisibility on the female protagonist by the early traditionalist male writers". Critics like Naana Banyiwe-Horne praises Nwapa's use of language and states that "The constant banter of women reveals character as much as it paints a comprehensive, credible, social canvas against which Efuru's life can be assessed". The critic, Christine Loflin is of the view that the use of dialogue in Efuru allows a sense of African feminism to emerge, free of Western imposed values (Jagne and Parekh 338).

The novel throws light on the significance of motherhood, influence on spirituality and superstition, igbo traditions and western influence on tradition.

The number of children in a marriage is considered as the measure of success or failure in a marriage. A woman's femininity is questioned or she may be considered either adulterous or cursed if she failed to conceive. Adizua's family members point out that, "two men do not live together" when they prompt him to take a second wife. According to them Efuru cannot be considered as a woman since she is childless. Efuru makes several contributions to the members of the community and enjoys helping humankind. So it is unjust to criticize her for not being a mother.

The Igbos are presented as very spiritual and superstitious. They view Efuru's barrenness as a curse like the infertility of crops. Such problems are fixed by visiting 'dibia'. The dibia is given gifts and he advises the visitors accordingly. Efuru attains a superior status when she was chosen by Uhamiri, the goddess of the Lake as one of her worshippers. There are instances of superstitions demonstrated by the fear of pregnant women crossing their legs. They believe that if the pregnant woman gets into contact with snails the children are not born with excessive saliva.

The novel presents several Igbo practices and beliefs. Nigeria is a diverse country with several ethnic groups like the Yoruba in the southwest, the Hausas in the north, and the Igbos in the southwest. Abandoned women and widows usually reside with the family of their son. Polygamy is prevalent in Igbo societies. A man is allowed to marry if his wife cannot bear children or if she is difficult to handle. "Taking a bath" or female circumcision is considered important before pregnancy. The novel also reflects western influences on Igbo tradition. The Igbos view Christianity as the root cause of their problems since it propagates the view that their "gods have no power". Thus people commit more crimes as they do not fear punishment. Several villagers including women attended schools and medicine lessened the significance of dibias. In the novel, Efuru sends several characters to hospital.

Another important aspect that is discussed in the novel is the significance of motherhood. The riverine Igbo community highly respected Uhamiri, the river goddess and prayed to her for children. The culture in Nigeria favoured women who had children particularly male children. In "Concept of Mammy water in Flora Nwapa's Novels", Sabine Jell-Bahlsen states that Ugwuta men and women pray to the divine pair of water deities, Uhamiri and Urashi, often called Mammywater (30). Nwapa in *Efuru* urges to have a more sympathetic attitude towards women who are childless. She analyses the condition of women in traditional Igbo society and examines their expected roles as wives and mothers within the community. Efuru who was childless and abandoned by her two husbands was marginalized by traditional society though she becomes a successful businesswoman who is called upon by many people in the community to assist them.

Chikwenye Ogunyemi finds that the first half of the novel attempts to find empowerment of Efuru through mothering in the community while the second half is "corrective and instructive" as she finds a peaceful existence as mother of the community (146). The novel deals with the ideological confusion, political awakening, material nurturing and spiritual development of Efuru (147).

The novel evaluates Efuru's choices and examines its consequences on self and society. Efuru met Adizua at a festival where people go to find prospective companions. Efuru is very much attracted to Adizua and insists to marry him. But Adizua tells her that he doesn't have enough money to pay the bride price. Efuru is determined and decides that they are "going to proclaim themselves married" (7). She moves to Adizua's house but her mother-in-law who learns about the situation is worried and declares, "You are welcome my daughter. But your father, what will you say to him?" (8). She is happy that her son has married the daughter of one of the most powerful men in the village. Efuru consoles her saying, "Leave that to me, I shall it myself" (8). She is happy to choose her own way without worrying about tradition. Mary Mears points out in her thesis that even the word choice "settle" indicates a type of bargaining. Obiora Nnaemeka refers to this type of action as "negotiating realities" (107). About a year later Efuru and Adizua earn enough money to pay the dowry. Later her father accepts Adizua's family and his request to marry Efuru. As Ogunyemi suggests, Efuru refuses to be bought by any man since it is part of her money that pays the dowry (147). Unlike most other women, Efuru refuses to be subdued and subtly maintains control of her life.

The novel also indicates the influence of west on tradition. People in the community find fault with Efuru's father's inaction. They point out, "Things are changing fast these days. These white people have imposed so much strain on our people" (11-12). Efuru's action indicates a sense of independence in several parts of the novel. She marries Adizua against tradition and decides to do trade instead of working in the farm with her husband. Many accuse her for not following her husband. Someone responds, "She refused to go to the farm. She is trading instead ... And I don't blame her. She is beautiful. You would think the woman of the lake is her mother" (12).

Though at first Adizua and Efuru have a successful marriage, Adizua deserts her later. He stays out all night and refuses to answer any questions about his actions. He abandons the marriage and does not even return for the funeral of his daughter, Ogonim. Efuru's mother-in-law asks Efuru to be patient and give Adizua time to mature: "Have patience, my daughter ... Everything will be all right. Don't mind my son. It is only youth that is worrying him and nothing else. He will soon realize what a fool he has been, and will come crawling to you ... Men are always like that" (51). Efuru analyzes the situation and realizes that he is going to another woman in Ndoni. She says, "There is a woman behind this indifference. A woman whose personality is greater than mine ... I must face facts ... Perhaps she is very beautiful and has long hair like mine ... Is she as stately as I am" (54). Efuru develops a new sense of self-worth and asks herself, "How long will this last? How long will I continue to tolerate him? There is a limit to human endurance. I am a human being. I am not a piece of wood ... I don't object to his marrying a second wife, but I do object to being relegated to the background" (53).

Efuru faces similar problems in her second marriage to Gilbert Eneberi. When Efuru decides to marry him, one of her friends is concerned that Gilbert has not married before. "And he has not married? Why has he not married?" (128). Efuru defends Gilbert by citing the influence of west on Nigerian customs and traditions. She says, "You forget that he went to school and that those who go to school do not marry early" (128). Efuru's marriage with Gilbert seemed to be a happy one until the issue of motherhood created problems in her life.

Efuru seemed disturbed after two years of her marriage with Adizua. She prays, "I am still young, surely God cannot deny me the joy of motherhood" (24). He mother-in-law states, "a child would come when God willed it" (24). Motherhood was necessary to obtain peace within and outside the society. A barren woman is ostracized from society. Efuru gave birth to Ogonim after two years of her marriage and when the marriage began to fail Ogonim too became ill. When Adizua abandoned Efuru and did not sleep with her for six months, Ogonim suddenly developed a fever, started having convulsions and eventually died. Efuru felt that the death of her daughter indicated the end of their marriage.

According to Carole Davies, one of the characteristics of African feminism is that a woman must be a mother at all cost, or her life is worthless. That is why Efuru questions her purpose in life when Ogonim dies. "Ogonim has killed me. My only child has killed me. Why should I live? ... Oh, my chi, why have you dealt with me in this way?" (73). Efuru felt that without a child of her own, she ought to die. As Barbara Christian points out, even though motherhood is revered, it is "universally imposed upon women as their sole identity, above all others" (212).

Motherhood is a major concern in Efuru's second marriage too. When Efuru is not pregnant even after two years of her marriage with Gilbert, women point out, "A woman, a wife for that matter, should not look glamorous all the time, and not fulfill [sic] the important function she is made to fulfill [sic]" (138). These words clearly indicate that the only purpose in a woman's life is to procreate. But Gilbert's mother, Amede declares that "Young people of this generation are different" (139). This indicates that western education has brought considerable change in society. Yet several women are completely upset that the couple is happy even without any child.

But their happy life did not last long and Gilbert neglects her and marries three times and has children by second and third wives as well as by another woman. Though Igbo tradition allowed a man to marry several times, Gilbert disobeys tradition by keeping his various affairs as a secret from Efuru. Gilbert who was western educated vacillates between colonial and traditional customs. When Gilbert reveals to his friend, Sunday that he has a child who is not Efuru's son, Sunday asks him to reveal the truth to Efuru before she finds it out from others. Gilbert replies, "I haven't the courage ... I am sure it is going to upset her" (190). Efuru is being forced to accept second place as a wife since she cannot bear children. When Gilbert's mother, Amede is asked about her son's several marriages, she replies that she does not want to interfere. The world is now of the "white people" and not of the Igbo "grand parents" (194).

Gilbert too abandons Efuru and does not return even for the funeral of her father, just like Adizua did not return for the funeral of their daughter. Efuru felt it as a "disgrace" and thought of killing herself (204). Later Gilbert informs Efuru that he was in jail for three months. Gilbert's disregard for Efuru is revealed through his several actions. He does not attend his father-in-law's funeral. He hides from Efuru the truth that he has a two-year-old son and does not give any explanation for why he was in jail. All this makes Efuru painfully realize her situation in life. She tells her doctor friend, "I am not an adulterous woman. So here I am. I have ended where I began- in my 'father's house'" (220).

Efuru's self analysis helps her to make confident decisions about her own life. Towards the end of the novel, Efuru realizes that Uhamiri cannot give her children because Uhamiri does not have children herself. In Efuru's dream she asks, "Can she give me children?" She felt, "Uhamiri smiled at me and asked me to come in. I went in [to her house under the water] ... Then she showed me all her riches" (146). Later, she realizes that the Uhamiri does not have children and concludes, "She cannot give me children, because she has not got children herself" (165). According to Patricia Hill Collins, women must place their thoughts, experiences and consciousness at the center of their interpretations. After a long time Efuru was finally able to sleep peacefully that night as she was at peace with herself. Efuru realized that she was not going to have children and that she can be happy only if she accepted that truth. According to Ogunyemi, Uhamiri allows Efuru to become a mother figure to the community through her wealth, charity, and nurturing of the community (154).

Women need to make choices in their lives that may not be in conformation with the traditional expectations. Efuru makes distinct choices in her life without pondering the effects her choices have on self and society.

Conclusion

Routledge International Encyclopaedia of Women (Vol. 2) defines empowerment as "a process that aims at creating the conditions for the self-determination of a particular people or group" (554). Barbara Christian points out in "The Race for Theory" that becoming empowered means "seeing oneself as capable of and having the right to determine one's life" (James and Sharpley-Whiting 21). This is, of course, different from the desire to achieve power.

Various groups of people have used empowerment to challenge social, economic, cultural, religious and other forms of subordination. Empowerment signifies the capability to change and is a means to mobilize people into action. The idea of women's empowerment has been significant in the evolution of women's movement. Paolo Freire put forward the idea of 'conscientization' which interested the early feminist theorists. Conscientization involves changes in beliefs, thoughts and ideologies. There is a redefinition of reality. It is consciousness-raising or a 'coming to awareness' (221 - 222). It questions power relations that support dominant ideologies, beliefs and cultures. The notion of changing consciousness helped in the revaluation of ideas and contributions made by the members of a subordinate group. Empowerment involved a change in consciousness. It is a process that the women themselves undergo and considered crucial by early feminists.

On many occasions 'coming to awareness' has been translated into action. The strategies employed include education, legal reform, protest and efforts to restrict social institutions. Women became aware of the ideologies and resources that controlled them and this has enabled them to make decisions that affect their own life. The movement for women's empowerment analyses the process of decision-making.

The movement for empowerment has a direct effect on the relations between people. It examines the changing power relations and focuses on how power is exercised. Many feminist critics have tried to reclaim the term 'power' by distinguishing between 'power over' and 'power to'. 'Power over' is understood as domination. 'Power to' is the ability to determine the course of one's life and actively to participate in society and culture" (*International Encyclopedia of Women,* Vol.2 1657). Charlotte Bunch and Samantha Frost write of an international feminist workshop sponsored by Asian and Pacific Centre for Women and Development (APCWD) in 1980 which began by defining women's power to control their own lives within and outside of the home as one of the fundamental goals of the women's movement. It notes that power is used not as a mode of domination over others, but as (a) a sense of internal strength and confidence to face life, (b) the right to determine our choices in life, (c) the ability to influence the social processes that affect our lives; and (d) an influence on the direction of social change. (555)

There are conflicts among various groups struggling for empowerment. Such conflicts have become a serious matter because the individual women or groups of women who have gained power have exercised it in the traditional sense of 'power over'.

Black feminist critics have adopted the concept of empowerment to improve the position of black women in society. Black women were made to feel inferior by white men, white women and black men. The writings of African women reveal their struggle to be independent. Men were physically stronger - the only reason for their 'superiority' to women. Women were made to feel inferior and their oppressors enjoyed humiliating them. Women's struggle is marked by individual as well as collective acts. Individual acts include leaving marriages or refusing to marry, and going to school in spite of the disapproval of family and society. Sometimes the struggle is taken forward by collective acts such as women coming together to share work, to make demands, to go on strike and so on. Women's energy should be directed towards their own benefit rather than to reinforce their subservience to patriarchy. In African societies where women have minimal power, their struggles are against unwanted marriages, malnutrition, exhaustion and work related diseases. Black women increasingly take active part in struggles for change. They fight for the right to make demands; they fight for reproductive control or for access to technological aids. They try to have some control over their lives, which would allow them to make further changes. They demand more opportunities for women in every area of life so that the segregation of women to the most menial, lowest paying jobs may be avoided. Their actions are oriented to increase the freedom of women and to preserve their rights. They fight against the deterioration of their status in the new society.

Black women's struggles have definitely led to changes. The changes, though small, are significant. Education and social conditioning help to form the ideals and behavior of women. Women should have reasonably high expectations about themselves. Lisa Leghorn and Katherine Parker opine that if women have low expectations of men, of their own lives and the options available to them, much of their energy would be directed towards figuring out ways of adapting to their environment. When they internalize the dominant view, they often sacrifice self-respect. When their self-respect and expectations rise they focus on the changes they need to make. In a patriarchal society, men control the sources of information available to women. Men restrict women's access to information. In African societies, educational opportunities are unequal. Through exposure, women, especially black women, learn that their conditions are different from those of other women. They may come to know about other women who have made changes in life in similar situations. They may hear about them through friends or through radio or television. In African culture, women's opportunities for education and sharing their experiences with other women are limited because in such societies women hold minimal power. When women's expectations are too low they failed to take advantage of the few opportunities that exist. When their expectations are too high their disillusionment can lead to bitterness.

Building networks and providing support to each other are necessities in the movement for empowerment of women. Women should have self-respect, hope and a sense of new options. Black women's sharing of the strategies for change and mutual support help them to realize that their situation is not isolated. Sharing their experiences gives them a sense of validation and empowerment. They will not feel powerless when faced with obstacles. Women have succeeded in building a network of other services like rape crisis centers, refuges for women in crises, and medical centers that are controlled by women.

In *Woman's Worth*, Lisa Leghorn and Katherine Parker quote from *I am not Meant to be Alone and Without You who Understand: Letters from Black Feminists*, in which Barbara Smith and Beverly Smith highlight the social networking among black feminists in different cities in the USA between 1972 and 1978. To quote (from Leghorn and Parker),

> Having written and received hundreds of letters, we realized that our correspondence was an important part of our black feminist activity. Letters have always been an important link for embattled groups, perhaps more so in the last century than in this one, before modern means of communication

were available. For women, letters have often been lifelines to each other, since traditionally we have had little control over where we live and have had little access to conventional media. Letters have provided an underground communications medium. [...] Most essentially, we write letters because we are apart. [..]. The letters have created an emotional support network among the women who shared them. The letters have also brought a network of individual black feminists together. [...] There is a sense in the letters that the writers are 'family'. One reason for the rich variety of the letters' contents is that we have so few places as black feminists to send our creations and to share ourselves ...

The antidote to isolation is networking, the creation of community. Networking is also an essential step in building our movement. [...]

One function the letters have served is to make us real to ourselves and to each other. To write a letter to another black woman who understands is to seek and find validation. The scope of this correspondence among black women shows how important we are to each other's lives. (219-220)

Education and the opportunity to share information give women hope and encouragement. Lisa Leghorn and Katherine Parker note that in some cases, women's participation in national liberation efforts has brought about changes in their status. Education, progressive legislation, a higher standard of living, access to wealth and freedom from violence gives them strength to fight for more changes.

Self-respect is the primary tool in women's struggles. This can be achieved through training and education. These provide women with skills with which to raise their income and standard of living, their self-respect and their networking ability. Education is the primary goal of women in many societies where women have only minimal power. Women's liberation involves self-recognition and recognition by others, including men. Self-recognition is the women's refusal to think of herself and other women as inferior to men. When women gain the recognition of men they are valued as persons and equal partners.

Education of women is essential for their empowerment. Studies reveal that over half of the world's women are illiterate. Eradicating illiteracy is possible by means of adult education. Illiteracy is a major problem faced by many post-colonial countries. Illiteracy is higher in the rural population than among urban groups. Illiteracy is a curse like malnutrition and the lack of basic human necessities in many African countries. Lack of education for women affects the entire family. It leads to poverty and affects the educational performance of children. Fertility rates are also significantly higher among poorly educated women.

Adult education centers aim at the development of work skills and career development. Adult education is often financed by religious groups and social and political organizations. The state typically plays only a minor role as a sponsor of adult education. The United States was the first industrialized society to legislate the Adult Education Act in 1966. It was followed by Sweden in 1967. Initially, women were excluded from adult education programs. The United Nations Educational Scientific and Cultural Organization (UNESCO) has worked for worldwide adult education since 1945. The organization aimed at women's participation in these programs.

Adult education enables black women to build their self-esteem and self-confidence. Education helps to empower them, gives them a sense of identity and purpose, and access to a network of friends and resources. It also gives them a new opportunity to complete their formal education, thereby enabling them to help solve the economic problems of the family. It increases their self-awareness and furthers their personal development. Such women can be of help in their children's education too. Women can also attend classes that help them perform better in traditional domestic roles such as child rearing, cooking and housekeeping. Likewise, they can keep themselves well informed about family planning, literacy and health. Rural women of Africa could be scientifically trained in the production and preparation of food and provided basic information about family planning, sanitation and nutrition.

Many adult education programs have been unsuccessful in ensuring that women complete the programs. Some women suffer from lack of financial resources to complete their education. Family responsibilities may also prevent women from persisting with such programs. Providing daycare centers, transportation, and/or domestic assistance may be of great help to these women. Women's educational achievement is a factor that determines the jobs they choose. Education provides women with basic skills which give them access to available resources and helps them to improve their status in a society where they are confronted by the oppression of racism, sexism, and social class.

Buchi Emecheta portrays in her novels the situation in African societies where there are laws that prohibit the education of women and exclude them from certain forms of work, thus rendering them powerless and unable to obtain divorces, abortion or even birth control. Laws are made by people in power to maintain their power. In many societies men have more power than women and make the laws that govern people's life. Their laws are a mechanism to maintain that power. Sometimes women are given legal power when they attain certain positions by merit and determination, but they may have to quit because of the force of sheer hostility. Men then point to such incidents as proof of women's inability to function in high positions.

Black women can be empowered by improving their working conditions and standard of living. Much of a woman's work has to be done at home and improvement in living conditions can lighten her workload. Women's groups can acquire a significant role if they adopt strategies that have achieved success in similar struggles elsewhere. To quote from Lisa Leghorn and Katherine Parker's account of the struggle of women in the United States,

> In the United States women formed groups and coalitions to mobilize their communities against the rapes and murders of women, such as the murders of black women in Boston in the winter of 1978 -79. Marches and street theatre focusing on issues of violence, as well as legislation to provide greater legal protection for women in crisis are also common. Increasingly, women are filing suits in rape and battering cases and winning large settlements. (234)

In modern African literary works we are witness to the subjugation of African women and to their aggressive struggle for greater visibility. African women continue to be subjugated even after the attainment of political freedom. Women have become more self-aware, confident and independent in spite of and perhaps because of hunger, war and physical, mental and economic oppression. In the works of the new African women writers, we find African women depicted as prophets, heroines, decision makers and challengers of their situation. One should not forget that African women had a significant role in society before the advent of the colonizers.

The colonized woman did not accept her situation passively. African women devised strategies to oppose the colonisers. Sometimes as in Ferdinand Oyono's *Houseboy* and Cheitch Hamidou Kani's *Ambiguous Adventure*, we find African women collaborating with the colonisers while opposing them. In *God's Bits of Wood*, Sembene Ousmane exposes the power and strength of women even under most difficult forms of oppression. Driven by pangs of hunger they become breadwinners. They are filled with rage when they realize that the white French man is the 'super power' controlling them. Ousmane here fictionalizes a historical event. The colonial government considers these African women as mere concubines.

They made themselves visible and faced death with immense courage. We find a similar development in the role of women in *A Grain of Wheat* by Ngugu Wa Thiong O'. As in *God's Bits of Wood* the presence of women at a union meeting is resented in Cheikh Hamidon Kane's *Ambiguous Adventure*. In *Ambiguous Adventure* the Most Royal lady wins a victory over the colonizers by 'co-operating' with the colonial government. Characters like Penda in *God's Bit of Wood*, Guthera in Nugget WA Thiong O's *Matigari,* Wanja in Ngugi's *Petals of Blood,* Kalisia and Ireyise in Oyono's Houseboy, and Jagua in Ekwensi's *Jagua Nana* are women who collaborate with the colonizers only to undermine their power. In Peter Abraham's *A Wreath for Udomo* and Francis Bebey's *Ashanti Doll* we find that the market women are a politically powerful group. Roopali Sircar refers to Ngugi's Waringo in *Devil on the Cross* and Achebe's Eunice (in the story "girls at war" in *Girls at War and Other Stories)* as shining examples of Revolutionary women who took the gun when they found the exploitation unbearable (215).

The image of the prostitute is a significant one in African literary works. Sircar refers to Khalid Kishtainy's claim that on the one hand the woman is presented as a symbol of corruption and decay and the dissipater of manhood and strength while on the other hand she is idealized as "the woman with a golden heart" and "the sacrificial lamb of the existing order" (215). Sircar lists a number of women characters who allow men to sexually use them – Ngugi's Wanja and Guthera, Rebeka Njau's Selena, Okotp Biteck's 'Malaya', Bessie Head's Life, Emecheta's Adja, Sembene Ousmane's Penda, Ama Ata Aidoo's Aunt Araba, Meja Mwangis' Wini, Oyone's Kalisia, Soyinka's 'Segi' and Ireyise and Ekwense's Konnie and Jagua Nana. These women are victims of society. Writers like Ngugi, Soyinka, Buchi Emecheta, Ama

Ata Aidoo and Sembene Ousmane point out the conditions that lead to prostitution. The women turn to prostitution because they are deprived of any other means of earning a living. They use their bodies to gain economic and sometimes political power. Ngugi's Waringa refuses to be sexually exploited once she is trained as a motor mechanic. Guthera in *Matigari* is a revolutionary who uses her sexual powers to release prisoners from jails. Male writers like Ekwense and Elechi Amandi have created prostitutes as images of corruption and decay. Ihuoma in Amadi's *The Concubine* and Jagua Nana in Cyprian Ekwense's *Jagua Nana* conform to the male belief that women are objects of male desire. In Wole Soyinka's *Konji's Harvest*, Segi rebels against president Konji. She organizes prostitutes into the Women's Auxillary Corps. While pretending to be loyal to Konji, they work to bring about his downfall.

In postcolonial Africa, black women recognize the black man as colonizer and exploiter. Buchi Emecheta's novel, *Destination Biafra* deals with war. It portrays the insecurity of black women when both enemy and fellow soldiers rape women in military attire. Debbie realises that neocolonialism could destroy her people. She becomes conscious of the limitations of her western education in the company of other women who remind each other of their traditional ways, their capabilities and their non-dependence on men for shelter and food.

Postcolonial African literary texts also highlight the corruption in postcolonial African states. Women are subjugated within the home. African women are mostly illiterate. Their feminist views are derived from their own experiences. They are deprived of any support by the traditional customs. Marriage and motherhood are used as tools to suppress them. Polygamy and clitoridectomy are still practiced even in urban Africa. Ebla in Nuruddin Frah's *From a Crooked Rib* severely condemns female circumcision. Literary works question the traditional favoring of sons. Males are accorded greater privileges in marriage. There is a loss of status in the case of females. Man is given the privilege to possess several women. This in turn leads to competition between them. This does not, however, disempower them completely. They learn through their sorrows to live without depending on men. Women cannot remain as passive victims. Bint Mahmoud in Tayeb Salih's Season *of Migration to the North* and Dikeledi in Bessie Head's *The Collector of Treasures and other Botswana Village Tales* castrate the men who forcibly have sex with them. Male writers like Tayeb Salih, Nuruddin Farah, Ngugi Wa Thiong O' and Sembene Ousmane are feminists who realized the oppression of black women and dealt with the concerns of black women. As Roopali Sircar has said,

> Ngugu Wa Thiong O' and Micero Mugo see the interconnectedness between race, class and sex oppression. Ngugi describes women as the most exploited and oppressed section of the entire working class, "exploited as workers and at home" and also by "backward elements in the culture, remnants of feudalism". As a result he says that he'd create a picture of a strong determined woman with a will to resist and struggle against the conditions of her present being. (221)

African literary texts reveal the ability of the African woman to survive and even to transcend their situation. They analyse their problems and challenge their situation and struggle for liberation.

Modern feminist critics have adopted the concept of empowerment to improve the position of women in society. Women cease to become victims. They recognize their potential to work individually and collectively to change the world in which they live. Women need to reflect on the idea of empowerment and recognize the goals of empowerment. Empowerment has the power to mobilize people to action and towards change. The novels of Buchi Emecheta and Flora

Nwapa draw attention to the fact that empowerment is essential for the liberation of women.

Works Cited

- Achebe, Chinua. *Things Fall Apart*. London: Heinemann, 1958 p.122. Print.
- Alcoff, Linda Martin. "Racism" *A Companion to Feminist Philosophy*. Eds. Alison M. Jaggar and Iris Marion Young. Oxford: Blackwell, 1998. Print.
- Ba, Mariamma. *So Long a Letter*. Trans. Modupe Thomas. London: Heinemann, 1981. Print.
- Baker, Houston. The Journey Back. Chicago : University of Chicago Press, 1980. Print.
- Bobo, Jacqueline. *Black Feminist Cultural Criticism*. Oxford: Blackwell, 2001. Print.
- Bone, Robert. *The Negro Novel in America*. 1958. New Haven, CT:Yale UP, 1972.Print.
- Bowlby, Rachel. "Breakfast in America: Uncle Tom's Cultural Histories" *Nation and Narration*. Ed. Homi K. Bhabha. London: Routledge, 1990. Print.
- Carby, Hazel. "White Woman Listen/Black Feminism and the Boundaries of Sisterhood in Centre for Contemporary Cultural Studies". *The Empire Strikes Back: Race and Racism in 70's Britain*. London: Hutchinson, 1982. Print.
- Davies, Carole Boyce. Introduction. Ngambika: Studies of Women in African Literature. Trenton, NJ: Africa World P, 1986. Print.

- ---. "Motherhood in the Works of Male and Female Igbo Writers: Achebe, Emecheta, Nwapa, and Nzekwu." Ngambika: Studies of Women in African Literature. Ed.Carole Davies and Anne Adams Graves. Trenton, NJ: Africa World P, 1986. Print.
- Eagleton, Mary, ed. *Feminist Literary Theory: A Reader*, 2nd ed. Oxford: Blackwell, 1996. Print.
- Emecheta, Buchi. *The Joys of Motherhood*. Oxford: Heinemann, 1994. Print.
- ---. *Second Class Citizen*. Oxford: Heinemann, 1994. Print.
- Frank, Katherine. "The Death of the Slave Girl: African Womanhood in the Novels of Buchi Emecheta". World Literature Written in English 21:2 (1982). Web. 3 July 2019.
- Friedan, Betty. *The Feminine Mystique*. Oxford: Penguin, 1963. Print.
- Holmes, Julie. Interview with Buchi Emecheta. "Just an 'Igbo' Woman". *The Voice*. 9 July 1996. Web. 25 Aug. 1996.
- Ibrahim, Huma. "Ontological Victimhood: 'Other' Bodies in Madness and Exile Toward a Third World Feminist Epistemology". *The Politics of (M)Othering – Womanhood, Identity and Resistance in African Literature*. Ed. Obioma Nnaemeka. London: Routledge, 1997. Print.
- Jagne, Sigha and Parekh, Pushpa. *Post colonial African Writers: A Bio bibliographical Source Book*. London: Routledge, 2014. Print.
- James and Sharpley-Whiting, ed. *The Black Feminist Reader*. Oxford: Blackwell, 2000. Print.
- Konadu, Asare. *Woman in Her Prime*. London: Heinemann, 1967. Print.

- Kramarae, Cheris and Dale Spender. *International Encyclopedia of Women - Global Women's Issues and Knowledge*, Vols. 1-4. New York: Routledge, 2000. Print.
- Leghorn, Lisa and Katherine Parker. *Woman's Worth: Sexual Economics and the World of Women.* Routledge and Kegan Paul: Boston, 1981. Print.
- Mc Dowell, Deborah. "Reading Family Matters". *Changing Our Own Words: Essays on Criticism, Theory and Writing by Black Women.* Ed. Cheryl Wall. New Brunswick: Rutgers UP, 1989. Print.
- Mears, Mary. *Choice and Discovery: An Analysis of Women and Culture in Flora Nwapa's Fiction.* Scholar Commons. 2009. Web. 8 July 2019.
- Nnaemeka, Obioma. "Feminism, Rebellious Women and Cultural Boundaries: Rereading Flora Nwapa and Her Compatriots." Research in African Literatures 26.2 (Summer 1995): 80-113.
- Nwapa, Flora. *Efuru.* London: Heinemann, 1966. Print.
- ---. *One is Enough.* Enugu, Nigeria: Jana Press, 1981. Print.
- O'Brien, John. Ed. *Interviews with Black Writers.* New York: Liveright, 1973. Print.
- Ogunyemi, Chikwenye Okonjo. Africa Wo/Man Palava: The Nigerian Novel by Women. Chicago: UP of Chicago, 1995. Print.
- Oluwele, Sophie. "Africa". *A Companion to Feminist Philosophy.* Ed. Alison M. Jaggar and Iris Marion Young. Oxford: Blackwell, 1998. Print.
- Sircar, Roopali. *The Twice Colonized: Women in African Literature.* Creative, New Delhi, 1995. Print.

- Spacks, Patricia Meyer. *The Female Imagination.* New York: Avon, 1976. Print.
- Stratton Florence. *Contemporary African Literature and the Politics of Gender,* London: Routledge, 1994. Print.
- Taylor, John V. *The Growth of the Church in Uganda: An Attempt of Understanding.* London: SCMP, 1958. Print.
- Turnbill, Colin M. *Africa and Change.* New York: Hofstra U and Knopf, 1973. Print.
- Umeh, Marie A., The Joys of Motherhood: Myth or Reality?" Digital Common @ Colby. Colby Library Quarterly, 18:1, March 1982. Web. 3 July 2019.
- Walker, Alice. "One Child of One's Own – An essay on Creativity". *Ms.* August 1979.
- ---. *The Color Purple.* London: Women's Press, 1992. Print.
- Ware, Vron. "Defining Forces". *The Postcolonial Question: Common Skies Divided Horizons.* Ed. Iain Chambers and Lidia Curti. London and New York: Routledge, 1996. Print.

SMART MOVES

India. USA.

p-ISBN: 978-81-940996-7-3

e-ISBM"978-81-940996-7-3